Many Mountains Moving

a
literary
journal
of
diverse
contemporary
voices

literature of spirituality

Cathy Capozzoli, Guest Editor

The Day When Mountains Move
Akiko Yosano

The day when mountains move has
   come.
Though I say this, nobody believes
   me.
Mountains sleep only for a little while
That once have been active in flames.
But even if you forgot it,
Just believe, people,
That all the women who slept
Now awake and move.

This poem was originally published in 1911 in *Seitō* ("Blue Stocking"), a Japanese literary magazine. It was reprinted from *The Burning Heart: Women Poets of Japan* (translated and edited by Kenneth Rexroth and Ikuko Atsumi, Seabury Press, 1977).

Guest Editor
CATHY CAPOZZOLI

Series Editor/Publisher
NAOMI HORII

Managing Director
HEATHER GRIMSHAW

Administrative Director
SUSAN BECKER

Cover Design
JOSEPH W. KRUSINSKI

Cover Typography
RICHARD JIVIDEN

Logo Design
CRAIG HANSEN

Technical Manager
JIM UBA

Webmaster
MICHAEL MCCOLE

Editorial/Production Assistants
SHANNON ARANCIO
HEATHER GRIMSHAW
MARGO MCCALL
JONATHAN PIERCE

Copyeditor
JESSICA MOSHER

Board of Directors
NAOMI HORII
GHADA ELTURK
JIM UBA
RENATE WOOD

2002

MANY MOUNTAINS MOVING (ISSN# 1080-6474; ISBN #1-886976-12-0)
is published semi-annually by MANY MOUNTAINS MOVING, Inc., a
501(c)(3) nonprofit organization. First North American Serial Rights. ©
MANY MOUNTAINS MOVING 2002. Many Mountains Moving, 420 22nd
Street, Boulder, CO 80302, U.S.A. Distributed by Small Press
Distribution. Indexed by The American Humanities Index (Albany, NY:
Whitston Publishing Co.) and The Index of American Periodical Verse
(Lanham, MD: Scarecrow Press).

CONTENTS

ABOUT THE CONTRIBUTORS
165

Special Thanks from the Guest Editor

The publication of this journal would not have been possible without the help of a great many friends and supporters. I would like to thank:

Anonymous and Anonymous
Susan Becker
Recd Bye
Willis Barnstone
Susie Cabell
Mary Agnes and Sam Capozzoli
Susan and John Cosgrove
Christopher Cross
Heather Grimshaw
Naomi Horii
Barbara Kraft
Joseph W. Krusinski
Dr. A. C. Labriola
Karol Paltsios and David Fisher
Jan Cook Reicher
Marsha Smith
Franny Stewart
Jim Uba
Liz Westerfield

To all of the contributors, artists, and photographers whose work appears on these pages, I am deeply grateful. Special thanks and dedication go to Mauri, and to the One and Only, who inspires and illumines us all.

Cathy Capozzoli
Guest Editor

Acknowledgments

We would like to thank the many friends and supporters whose contributions and subscriptions have made this issue possible. Special thanks are due to the following:

Patrons
Susan and Jim Bell
Chuck Hebert
Pam Swanson
Vernie and Arthur Ourieff
Celestial Seasonings

Donors
Nancy and Chet Volpe

Supporting Subscribers
Rachel Dacus
William Marshall, Jr.

Organizational Donors
We gratefully acknowledge support from the **Arts and Humanities Assembly of Boulder County (AHAB)** through the AHAB/Neodata Endowment. We are grateful for marketing support from the **Council of Literary Magazines and Presses** and from **Small Press Distribution** through the New Readers for New Writers Program. Funded in part by a grant from the **Boulder Arts Commission**, an agency of the Boulder City Council. Thank you to the **SCFD** for funding our Literature of Spirituality reading series. Also, we would like to thank Margaret Maupin and the Tattered Cover; Boulder Bookstore; James Lough of *The Rocky Mountain News*; Common Grounds of Denver; and the Women's Art Center—for their support in hosting Many Mountains Moving readings.

Finally, many thanks to our readers, who are dedicated to opening an exchange among cultures through art and literature.

Many Mountains Moving, Inc. is a 501(c)(3) nonprofit organization. If you wish to make a tax-deductible contribution, or are affiliated with an organization that might like to make a tax-deductible contribution, please contact the office, please contact us at 303-545-9942 or e-mail us at mmm@mmminc.org.

Preface: The Spiritual and the Literary
Cathy Capozzoli

O nourishing river
Mother of all that is written
Inspire fluent, truthful words.
May I discover the sacred river of wisdom within.
— *Invocation of Saraswati, the Hindu*
Goddess of Inspiration

Did you ever experience a moment of great clarity, in which you know that all this really is part of something much, much more? Have you ever read something that immediately takes you to a place of deep and abiding truth? If the language of the soul is the vibration of the universe, the pages of this journal are filled with creative works attempting to capture it.

Since the time long ago when oral traditions of the world shifted to written traditions, writers have tried to capture these vibrations in words, translations from the realm of concept or experience to the realm of language. In turn, the seekers and faithful have sought the literature of the spirit for insight and meaning.

Creative writing and literature are important in every religious tradition as expressions of the divine. Every world faith tradition has a body of literary works, beyond the sacred texts, to which seekers turn for inspiration.

In the Tibetan Buddhist tradition, for example, poetry has long been one of the primary means of expressing spiritual experience. Many also have looked to the Hindu poet-saints of India to nourish the heart. Those works, as well as the ones on these pages, bravely seek to describe that which transcends all, within the inherent limits and inadequacies of our language.

For some writers, no matter what the topic, writing is a sacred practice in itself. Other writers find divinity in writing about their own spiritual concepts and experiences. While the spiritual journey is personal, it also is universal. We see ourselves in that which is personal to another because of the common bond that unites us all as humans. Divinity is wherever we are. Further, the study of the sacred texts of the world's religions will reveal that many of the core teachings are similar across faith traditions. At the center of it all, we all are longing for and seeking the same God. The inner, spiritual life, as Thomas Moore calls it, is the lining of the deep soul. It's the higher presence, the beyond, the other, God, or what the Hindus call "that" or "not this." These writers have tried to define what is deeper than deep, within or without a theology.

The works on the pages of this journal correspond to a wide number of faith traditions. They represent a wide number of genres within creative writing. We have poems, short fiction, essays, prayers, even a ghazal — a poem-song in the tradition of ancient Persia. We have Buddhism, Hinduism, Christianity in all of its facets, Judaism, and the spiritual that is not connected with any faith tradition.

Does the spiritual exist? Some would argue. Does spiritual literature exist? Yes, and there is a vigorous, growing interest in it. How would we tell the difference between sacred versus secular writing? It all begs a larger question. Is everything spiritual? Yes. Are all acts, including writing, spiritual? As my yoga teacher says, "You can use the knife to cut the fruit or cut a throat." Is the cut throat a spiritual act? Events in our world call us to contemplate this. Somehow the timeless has become more timely. With this, the works in this collection have an even stronger voice: one that brings unity rather than distance. We hear the voice of the spirit speak for all humanity.

For here and now, in these pages, allow us to say that spiritual literature is literature that directly addresses the spiritual. May we all have inspiration.

Contemplations
on the Literature of Spirituality

On the Sacred and the Profane
Martin Scott

Given the world's pleasures and agonies, any God worth contemplating should have a fetish for the profane. The Asian deities, in their varied depictions, seen to come fully equipped with the irony to enjoy the practices they (sometimes) keep outside the temple, and the venerable Yahweh doesn't shrink from shocking acts of violence. Even Jesus, if the Gospel of John can be believed, turned the water into wine, facilitating the further inebriation of a sorry group of already-sloshed party goers.

Clearly we cannot get very far into the literature of the sacred without having to deal with the profane. All the fleshly imagery can be taken as metaphors for spiritual truths, but the spirit needs the flesh to speak. Temples are built — and texts written — by profane bodies subject to the very desires and processes transcended by religion.

In most spiritual narrative, one moves from the profane to the sacred, as in conversion texts such as Augustine's Confessions. But one can also go the opposite direction, as in Thomas Paine's anticonversion to Reason, or de Sade's books. In metaphorical-based texts, the emphasis is not upon movement of the soul but a moment of exalted perception: One discovers the sacred hiding in the profane (Whitman or the Bhagavad Gita) or one discovers the profane hiding in the sacred (Neitschze or Bataille). These four patterns of development are arcs in the spiraling growth of the individual and the species. The sacred and profane are, perhaps, simply different faces of the same die.

The Modern Epistle
Rosemerry Wahtola Trommer

Over time, *epistle* has come to be interpreted almost exclusively in its spiritual sense, referring to the letters of the apostles. In its origin, however, an epistle is any communication made to an absent person in writing. In ancient times, it specifically referred to letters that ranked as "literary productions" — writings intended for the public that were addressed to a body of people.

In this sense, all of literature is epistolary. It's no coincidence that academicians still refer to the art of writing as "letters."

Contemporary literature — the collection of modern epistles — is seldom construed to be spiritual. But literary writing doesn't need to be *about* spirituality in order to *be* spiritual. The act of writing for an audience is spiritual in and of itself.

Spirit is literally the animating or vital principal in man and woman that gives them life. Spirit in literature is the animating or vital principal that man or woman gives to an idea. Writing literature is an attempt to create meaning. It is an effort to express joy, fear, love, hate — all the vital drives that animate woman and man. It is a physical manifestation of the invisible. It is an endeavor to make connections.

In this sense, all letters can be interpreted as spiritual writings, whether they are in the Bible or in the canon.

An Old Metaphor Gone Quantum

Keith Abbott

In his Mountains and Water Sutra, the thirteenth-century Zen Master Dogen anticipated the insights of twentieth-century physics when he wrote, "One day (or suddenly) water sees water." This metaphor relates to his notion that perception is not reserved for sentient beings, because there is no such thing as nonsentient beings (the term is an oxymoron at its metaphysically logical frontier, a species of useful nonsense inside its practical circumference). To be seen involves a reaction on the part of both viewer and viewee, then evidences an interaction. Hence, quantum physics: to subject any element to even passive experimental observation changes that element and you and creates a third thing; the result: element-you-observation.

"Mr. Perrier meet Mrs. Tap Water" would be one way to cast this into a fiercely comic and class distinctive dramatic mode, a la Jane Austen. The result would be "Love At First Sight" binding all three into a new experience. Or, let's call it "Gulp."

Awareness that water is aware of you can radically change a person's life for the best, as it should engender, in Dogen's constant term, "a thorough examination." There is in his watery sentence the promise of humility and compassion and grace. Grace because water moves so beautifully. Kinship and identification with such a beauty can only improve the hours.

An Answer, a Song, a Pile of Stones

Jeff Gundy

I have been increasingly drawn toward poems that deal with things of the spirit while resisting mere dogma or description. This impulse stems from one of my few certainties: that whatever it is that I worship —

call it the spirit of beauty and truth and justice and mercy that guides us through the world—it is bigger, older, wilder, stranger than we will ever understand or fully reckon. The rational mind and the senses offer us categories and information, the soul has its leanings and intuitions, much wisdom lives in books and human community, but what we call God is outside and inside them all, both farther and nearer than we can truly reach.

What might a poem do, then? Perhaps merely register our longing, invoke one place and time when the world opened for a moment. Perhaps offer a glimpse, a touch, a breeze from some other place. At best mere metaphor, mere words—while what the spirit says is mostly not in words, mostly not "said" at all. Could a poem be like the transcription of the cardinal's song, not an equivalent, but a record? Or an answer, another song? Or, perhaps, a small pile of stones left by a clear lake to say yes, we were here, and we took something away that we did not have to carry in our hands or on our backs.

The Spirituality of Literature
Judith Lavezzi

What is the Spirituality of Literature about? Is the fabric of human life woven throughout with the divine? Is literature an explanation of the individual spiritual experience or is it the attempt to extricate from humanity's most persistent concerns a measure of meaning and purpose using written form to shrink the unknowable abyss into controllable bits of ponderables? Is it an elevation of the mundane?

Living, Dying, Loving, Grieving, Surviving, Realizing, Feeling, Fearing, Taking, Looking, Sensing, Touching, Praying, Hurting, Forgiving, Stretching, Trying, Leaving.

These are the actions of a Human Being. Do they separate into the spiritual versus the physical? Is there a separation? Where I exist, does spirituality exist?

Metaphor and the Spiritual Life
Kate McHenry

For a poet, to say God is Poet might at first express similarity. But the force of metaphor can shift; from another perspective the same term expresses enormous difference: "I am to God as this writing on paper is to me."

It is the nature of metaphors to wear, and need replacement. The journey toward God is a process of widening horizons. One operates within a certain frame of reference, whose border one calls God. But something happens to break the frame. It feels like disaster, but it turns out God is still there. One lives in this larger understanding until it too is strained and must be broken.

Growing toward God is a series of larger boxes. God is always outside the box.

"Upstart Crow"
Painting by Keith Abbott

Prologue
Leonard Borenstein

The Tenant

If you tell me
the soul I bear
was always meant
for me,
why does my body fight
the way it fits?

Koan
Meredith McGhan

Of muse and god
one echoes in the void,
one is the void.

It's not that everything you hold
is illusion, it's
the holding.

North of Oz
Lucy Aron

Once you stumbled upon the place and now burn
holes in your shoes to find it again. From Maine
to Madagascar, compass in pocket, coordinates
inscribed on your brain like the name of a firstborn,
you trek with a hunger that feels encoded in your DNA
for one glimpse.
                But did you remember
              to toss away
                  your gear?

"Hand"
Photo by Thomas E. Kennedy

Untitled

John Vieira

you get a glimpse
of it like never

before of infinity
or eternity maybe

there's no name for
it here & it lasts

but a long instant
of life & you use

the rest of your
times figuring how

to beckon it back
into this living

into your awareness
into the sunny room

*

when we
open our
hearts like
a redwood

light pours
out &
in so
that we

expand to
suffer all
the winds
thru time

& space
never letting
up because
why would

we &
let God
our everlasting
axis down?

Praying in Place
Elizabeth Andrew

Venus is rising. From my living room window, I spot her hovering over a street lamp in the east. The corner grocery parking lot glows an unearthly orange; the city's haze blurs the night sky, but still, it's clear enough to see earth's sister planet, the goddess of beauty. It is said she moves in radiant light. She pierces her way into my morning, putting the darkness of my house in perspective. I light a candle; I bend to my knees. My candle is small, swallowed up by looming shadows. But Venus is even smaller in the enormity of space. There's so much emptiness out there! No wonder cities huddle under clouds of artificial light. The night sky is full of enough darkness that we might at any time slip off the earth's surface and fall forever heavenward.

I kneel before my window the same way that my grandmother used to kneel before bed—with great deliberation, as though her body knew humility, and she simply yielded to it. I kneel in a small circle of candlelight, the house an expansive cavern at my back. Perhaps by taking time, I can learn to live with all this emptiness. I want a quiet mind. I want to learn how to pray. The day, with its many complicated hours, waits across the street, behind rows of houses and below the horizon. My house waits, too, its walls not yet solid with sunlight, its windows not yet alive with seeing. Venus, "who steals away even the wits of the wise," is rising. I submit myself to gravity and the dangerous stillness of the present moment.

I know my grandmother knelt before bed because I peeked one night when I was little. My grandparents had matching twin beds, one two inches taller than the other to accommodate their respective heights, with real springs built into the frames. My grandfather died when I was seven, and after that, whenever we came to visit, my grandmother moved to the taller bed against the wall, giving me, her eldest grandchild, her own bed. Did she think Gramps' bed would frighten me? Or was it just harder for me to climb into? Grandma's bed felt the same as my bed at home, only I was aware that I was sleeping on air—I could hang my head over the edge and see between the metal curly-cues under the mattress.

Sent to bed long before the adults, I lay awake watching shadows from the streetlight and elm limbs play across the ceiling. The springs beneath me squeaked when I shifted. In the closet to my right, the mirror glinted above my grandmother's dressing table. I knew that tucked into its frame were photographs of us grandchildren and the crumpled drawings we'd sent her. My one-year-old hand print, pressed in clay, hung on the wall. From downstairs came the rattle of backgammon dice and low murmur of family, minus my grandfather's husky voice.

A strange sensation overcame me before sleep, not only then but every night when I was young. I fell backwards, turning heels over head through the utter blackness of space. There was no earth, no light, no point of reference; just a slow, effortless back-dive through nothing. I was the hands of a great clock turning backward in time, only I was affixed to no face—there was nothing stationary with which to measure distance. It was both pleasurable and terrifying. I gripped the sheets in an attempt to stay attached to the bed. At Grandma's that night, I first spun backward through the recesses of the universe, then fell asleep.

Past midnight she tiptoed into the room, waking me. I lay still. She sat at the dressing table beside me to remove her nylons, and suddenly it occurred to me that she missed Gramps. Were I to roll over, Grandma's thoughts would first go to him. Gramps should be the one watching her step out of her wool skirt and straight-pin it to the hanger, not me. Her body was pale, lumpy at the waist. She gathered the flannel of her nightgown from the hem up until the neckline was at her thumbs, and then slipped it over her head. It fell lightly against her skin. Walking over to Gramps' bed, she eased her body down, slowly, to her knees.

I held my breath. I knew prayer to be something we recited in church, said while holding hands around the dinner table, or shared with Mommy briefly before bed—a communal occurrence, spoken with and for other people. That people might offer up a personal prayer had never occurred to me. The picture books in Sunday school showed angelic children kneeling the way my grandmother knelt, at a bedside looking toward heaven, but I had never actually witnessed it. In reality it was different—more severe, more substantial. The night around me reeled. Through my slitted eyes, I sensed the privacy that my grandmother assumed in my sleeping presence. Death had left an extra, empty bed in the room. My grandmother knelt before it and before the window which was open to the night sky. *Something magnificent is out there*, I thought— *something worthy and awesome*. I squeezed my eyes shut so as not to see.

They say that if you die leaving unburned candles in your home, it's a sign of a life not fully lived. I am burning my candles; I am learning to live each moment as though it's my last. Here in the quiet depths of the morning, I forgo kneeling to lie on my back. Through the piano window high on the southern wall the stars are beginning to blur. I try to recreate my childhood experience of turning backward in bed. I want my prayer to be as complete and unrestrained as that sensation. My imagination conjures up the gradual lowering of the pillow and raising of my feet; I picture myself spinning through the darkness as though I'm a corpse released from a starship: heels over head floating slow motion through the great void. But my gut fails to believe it. I am exerting too much effort. When I was a girl, the sensation came unbidden, something which happened to me rather than something I made happen. It was a pre-birth memory: freeing, connective.

At this point in my life, what's on the other side of death comes not as memory but as premonition: *Something mighty is out there*. Venus is a point of light couched in a vast amount of darkness. Each of our lives is like Venus—a bundle of activity hurtling through a universe billions of light-years wide. Do I look for mightiness in the specks of light, or in the space between? This planet I've got my back against is a miraculous anomaly. Perhaps there are a great many such blips in the void, but, in proportion to the entirety, they are an "insignificant number," which my high school chemistry teacher defined as the weight of ashes in the armrests of an airplane compared with the weight of the whole. Even if there are a thousand other life-supporting planets out there, the breadth of this dark universe is excessive in proportion. What is the purpose of so much nothingness? The quantity stuns me.

Yet each morning I kneel before it. Whatever I suspect is out there I want to welcome into my home and heart. Contemporary physicists call space a "creative vacuum;" in order to support the explosion and implosion of energy which fuels life, a tremendous amount of nothingness is necessary. Without it there would be no planetary existence, no interplay between stars. Space is a reservoir empty enough to contain limitless possibility. Big bang: Something comes from nothing. It's a creation story harder to believe than seven days and seven nights.

Even so, it's not all that different. *In the beginning God created the heavens and the earth. The earth was without form and void, and the darkness was upon the face of the deep; and the Spirit of God was moving over the face of the waters*. This morning and every morning, the earth is again without form. Darkness is upon my face. I am my grandmother, with her back to a child and her eyes on the heavens. With every prayer I step nearer to death.

I was seven when my grandfather had the heart attack that killed him. A heavy smoker in his earlier years, Gramps had had a laryngectomy about the time I was born, and so his gruff voice emerged from the wrong place—a fact that frightened me. Still, no one else read Brer Rabbit with such fine inflection. I curled up on his lap and the strange, southern animals, full of chatter and misadventure, became most alive.

My family was moving from Los Angeles back to Tarrytown, New York, when we stopped in Utica to visit the grandparents. It was a homecoming—the errant Andrew family, not fit for west-coast living after all, returning to where we belonged. Gramps wasn't feeling well, but not bad enough to spoil the party. Until he stumbled down the stairs early Saturday afternoon with a pain in his chest.

I sat on the living room carpet, a backgammon board opened expectantly in front of me. I was still young enough that adults were inexplicable, their movements a constant surprise. Only when I heard fear in Gramps' voice did it register that this was not right, that he was in danger—that our game would not happen after all. Suddenly, the house was full of activity. I sat, erased momentarily from my parents' concern, the panic in the air absorbed into my hummingbird heartbeat and wide eyes. In a flurry of bad judgment, the adults got Gramps into our yellow Dodge and my father drove off, depending on Gramps for directions to the nearest hospital. Only women remained: Grandma and Mommy sitting stiffly on the sofa, my sister and I sprawled on the floor. The afternoon sun streamed through the closed windows until the house was stifling. Four of us strained against the forces of gravity, praying for the impossible.

"Can't we *please* play a game?" I asked, trying to break the tension. It was my grandfather inside of me who was restless, who knew that waiting would make no difference. A game of cards redeems all idleness. The silence continued for a minute, and then my mother said, "You can go get a game."

I stepped over the backgammon board, opened for Gramps and best left untouched. Out on the porch I found a three-dimensional version of tic-tac-toe, whose pieces rattled obtrusively when I carried the box in. Three clear plastic squares stacked on thin legs, unstable on top of the wall-to-wall carpeting. The sun highlighted dust motes in the air and shone bluntly through the layered panes. Blue and red checker pieces felt too light in my palm. I tossed them around, placing them randomly on the clear high-rise. I knew no one would play with me.

Forever passed, and then the phone rang. Gramps had passed out in the car. My father had flagged down a tow truck, which flashed its lights and raced through stop signs down Genesee Street. Gramps died shortly after they arrived at the hospital. My mother hung up the phone in the kitchen and conveyed this news to us with her hands limp at her sides. The medical staff harvested his eyes, she said. Pa wanted that, she said. Her tears began as the message sank in. Grandma wept softly on the sofa. I dismantled my transparent, sunlit tower, wondering what would happen to Gramps' eyes when they were no longer inside of his body.

Prayer is rarely what we expect. At first there's Venus, but then the whole house begins to unfold. The wall facing the east windows now exists; it looms and shifts, lighter than the north and south walls by a single degree. The change is so gradual, I don't notice until it's happened—the doorway to the kitchen gains dimension, the glass covering artwork glows. I realize once again that I have a body and it is solid, my knees hurt, and my hands are pulsing. Is this prayer? From my back, I gaze up through the piano window and can extrapolate the whole morning sky beyond my rooftop. It's a broad, concave expanse arching over the city, suddenly silver, suddenly blue. Venus is gone. Or she is there, but I grieve her visible reminder, the beam from a lighthouse warning me of the coastline. This day I'm sailing on is a vast, heaving ocean.

Where, after all, are Gramps' eyes? As a girl, I imagined them inside the sockets of a young woman's face, formerly blind but given sight by a dead man. The world through his eyes (through any eyes at all) must have seemed a stunning place. Today I suspect that, when we live each moment as though it's our last, our lenses are tainted with mortality. Sight, for that woman and for those who look, however briefly, through the ends of things, puts light in the perspective of darkness. Death is a constant companion. At any point, we might reel heels over head through nothingness, spilling out of our busy lives into a place of utmost quiet.

This is what I want in prayer and what I most fear. Prayer is a headlong plunge into the unknown; it is an ego death, a taste of void. Every morning it is the same: the cavernous emptiness around me filling with light, my heart straining for its pulse to be heard by the world, words spiraling in my head. As with the universe, so it is with prayer: Before there is something there first must be nothing. I strive for openness, that spirit might make its wild and unwieldy entrance. I may never again feel the sensation of spinning backward, but occasionally—blessed moment!—my heart leaps. It fills the living room, indistinguishable from sunlight.

You know what hour it is, how it is full time now for you to wake from sleep. Insidious, my Christian upbringing surfaces, shaping this morning. *For salvation is nearer to us now than when we first believed; the night is far gone, the day is at hand.* I imagine those early Christians, reprimanded by Paul to believe that the edge of existence was close. For them there was no literal tomorrow. Proceeding with life must have seemed impossible. *Now* was all that was left for being merry; why not cast off possessions and fling oneself into revelry?

But then time went on and on, and the end, as the believers perceived it (even as we perceive it now, scoffing at their naiveté), never came. Paul reprimanded his flock to return to work lest the pagans consider them lazy. God will appear at any moment, he said, but still, get on with life.

Scientists tell us that each ounce of matter in the universe has its origin at a single point, dense and explosive; the eyes in my skull are made of star dust. Perhaps Paul was right after all, and the opposite is true: The end is part and parcel of every instant. What awaits us after death—salvation, or life after reincarnated life, or the composting humus of a grave—already has arrived, and we contain it in our bodies. In prayer, then, we sit with origins and end times. No wonder I fear prayer's free-fall more than I long for it. No wonder my mind fills with chattering distraction.

Wakefulness isn't meant for a later date. Nor is wellness, nor "deliverance to a place of safe-keeping," as the Greeks defined salvation. Our creative lives—the lives we've always wanted, full of revelry and rejoicing and the intricate textures of grief, the lives of potential fulfilled, time fattened with intention; they are meant for now. Salvation is this sun warming my skin. Salvation is the halo of light that fills the earth's atmosphere every morning. Out of all that dark and emptiness, another day is born. It's an immaculate conception.

The day is at hand. I rise. I blow out my candle, irrelevant with all this sunlight. Venus, too, has long since been obliterated. In western cultures, she is the morning star, the bearer of light, the ruler of springtime, but in the east, the planet is male, autumnal, the color of death. Daytime arrives with Venus's demise. During my grandfather's memorial service, I swung my stockinged legs and drew with a pew pencil on the cover of the church bulletin. The drawing was of the place I imagined Gramps had gone: a cemetery with flowers and bluebirds and a spiky sun. The cross that was my grandfather's grave said "Quentin Fischer: A Very Good Man."

If death is the ultimate emptiness, it is also the place of ultimate creation. My candle's extinguished flame is another death from which morning expands in all directions. I stretch myself up then out, behind then before. I emerge from the cavity of prayer into another ordinary day. In reality, Gramps was cremated, his ashes saved to stir with my grandmother's and scatter to the wind. His body will mix with a body he loved. My prayer now rises in smoky wisps the same way I imagine their ashes will, released into the fabric of the universe.

The Raveling Back into the Text of Her Genesis
Mary Krane Derr

How I do forget
how we each mistake
our primordial
ultimate
Self

for the later rendings of it;

how each of us calls
the dumb
shriveled
tatters

of our ripped-up
remembering
Alpha over here,
Omega over there.

Yet whenever
I am raveled
back and back
down my umbilicus
before even
the naming
of any such names
into the text
of my Genesis

before anything
has torn at or snipped off
any vector of my burgeoning —

I am found to be
what I always am,
a daughter-surge
of new limb unfurling
out from the loose deep swaddle of glow
that is God's own

Infinity of Womb:

the glow that still
filters
warmly

through my translucent
unbending
hands

when I float them up strongly
to each glad day,

the freshly
eternal
seamless
surprise

that what
we can all
remember

is every bit
true:

we are everyone
in every split atom
of our incandescent flesh
furled and knit
and rolled together out

from an old,
the oldest
of any
Sun

The Restoration
Kris Christensen

When the last tree crumbled we used old women
for joists and rafters, for cantilevers and rib-shaped
cathedral beams, and in bones leached brittle
found the eggshell's perfect strength.
Former gymnasts leapt into archways.
Ancient waitresses balanced rooftops
on narrow arms. All winter
old women warmed floorboards, breath
knocking soft in the walls. They formed towers
and when earthquakes came
the women remembered dancing and simply
swayed. Standing for centuries
they met storms like lovers, crippled feet
anchored deep in the earth.

And there were old women named Amber
and Tiffany, women with intricate tattoos
who braced the domes of sanctuaries
where their withered roses and butterflies,
dolphins and shrunken snakes were mistaken
for Jesus' face. Old men came back to the churches
to witness the transfiguration—arthritic twists of limbs,
the talon hands, the terrifying breasts—all suspended,
bird-like above the Virgin's lead shores.
The old men stood enraptured by all
they had lost, stunned as if falling
from the memory of a thigh, and they wept
the deep slow tears of the saved.

St. Thomas Aquinas and the Brahma Bulls
Andrea Carter Brown

After the cowgirls' cloverleaf competition
and a family of four jumps in and out
of a rope circle suspended in the air
at their knees to "God Bless America,"
a man in pink and purple satin leads six
white bulls with dinner plates growing
straight up between their shoulders into
the ring. Nose to tail they trot two by two
around him, then, *wonder of wonders*,
three abreast followed quickly by the pièce
de résistance: with whip and prod and God
only knows what else, he coaxes these bulls
up onto stools no larger than their hooves
where they teeter as he bows to the ground.

The first time I saw "La Conquistadora"
she wore black and that fish eye expression
mothers have meaning *you can do no right*.
So while others lit candles and prayed, I told
her off and went my way. But faith requires
only need. Those who seek, the book says,
shall find. After the rodeo I find myself
again before her, that forbidding gaze grown
five years later more fitting. May bitterness
not poison my heart. The plea of all vanquished
is good enough for me. Some may care how many
angels can dance on the head of a pin; give
me St. Francis any day, his bare feet planted
on earth, his punctured palms lifted in submission.

All Souls
David Chura

"Rest For All Who Enter Here." The metal banner with the letters cut out like a stencil so that the words were colored blue or gray depending on the day arched across two poles at the entrance to St. Nicholas cemetery. Although it was written in Ukrainian, which I could not read, I knew what it promised, and it was, for my father and for me, the place for an ironic rest, not the rest of sleep or death, but the pause between the notes of a somber symphony.

My mother would announce, right after mass on Father's Day, what my brothers and I already knew: that we were going to the cemetery to visit the graves of my father's parents.

My father could read that stenciled sign. I had seen the small cracked leather prayer book held shut by a tarnished clasp he received at his First Holy Communion. Its pages were filled with words that didn't look quite right. Whenever we drove by St. Nicholas School, my mother would tell us how our father had had to go there every day after school (he went to public school since his family was poor) and study Ukrainian for hours in the basement. But I never heard my father speak Ukrainian, nor speak about those long afternoons. By the time I came along, he seemed to have eschewed language all together.

I would walk close behind my parents as they made their way toward the family plot at the back of the cemetery, ardent to hear my father speak the litany of names of his relatives and old family friends buried in the various plots we passed. Ordinarily he was a fast walker, keeping a pace none of us, sons or wife, could keep up with. But on those Sundays, he walked unhurriedly, deliberate but curiously tranquil, with none of his usual impatience. He seemed almost to welcome our presence. There, in that dry field, his world grew more expansive and circumscribed in turn. All the world he knew as a youngster now lay beneath his feet. Yet, at the same time, its chain-linked confines made it seem, for once, manageable.

How strange to hear my father speak words like "cousin" or "uncle" as he pointed out the various markers to my mother. The only uncles and cousins I knew were nowhere close to death. He spoke to my mother about the dead the way she talked to us about her relatives from "up north" or about her old girlfriends. Stranger to hear him whisper "sister" as he stooped over to pull out ribbons of crab grass edging up a gravestone marked "Martell." My mother clung to his arm as though to hold him back from disappearing into the ground.

Mary, my father's oldest sister, died a young married woman of cancer. "Your father adored her," my mother would tell us. It did not seem incredible, seeing him bent over that grave, clearing it of grass and polishing the gray marble stone with his handkerchief.

None of us was in a hurry those Sundays, except perhaps Walter who was old enough to have a life of his own. He knew enough not to complain and knew enough not to presume too much of the more languid, soft man my father appeared to become under the influence of sun, stone, and family stories. Instead, he waited as patiently as his knotted necktie let him. Dennis exhausted himself in the way of all baby animals, running back and forth between my parents and the grave marker.

There, gathered at our family headstone, was the only place where I felt like we were a family, where I felt like my father's son. Settled into a crescent in front of the graves, we knelt down, almost simultaneously, as though we had no choice. My eyes were pulled to the names chiseled into the stone: Euphemia and Peter, my father's parents, Delores, his sister, Stephen, his brother. These were ghosts that haunted my father, and their lives were a big part of the secret lore of my childhood. At times, it was hard to remember that these people whom my mother told us about had really existed. But their names etched there in stone made her stories plausible. Their lives were held firm by that monument like memory itself. And I knew how heavily that stone and those memories hung on my father's neck.

Although Delores and Stephen were my father's youngest siblings, I never thought of them as aunt and uncle. To me they were perpetual children. Both were retarded, the weakest links in that long chain of children, ten in all, that my grandmother gave my grandfather. I had no idea what "retarded" meant. There were no retarded children in my school. I imagined that, since Delores and Stephen were children and children were always at fault, they had done something wrong.

"Delores," she said, "was a Mongoloid," which sounded both foreign and like a scary disease. Although Delores got sick a lot, my grandmother refused to put her in an institution, even though caring for Delores wore her out. "Your father and your aunts and uncles all helped to take care of her." She told us, "When Delores was real small, your father loved to pull her in this rusty old wagon he had up and down 23rd Street. When she would get bronchitis, or even worse, pneumonia, your father would sit up all night with your grandmother, watching over both of them." Delores finally died at sixteen. I was never sure which was harder for me to believe: that I really had had an aunt who sounded like a cross between a monster and a cuddly doll or that my father was capable of such gentleness and caring.

Decades later, when my brother, Walter, and his wife, Betty Jane, became foster parents for a seven-year-old Down Syndrome girl named Kimberly, I saw my father show more warmth and love to that straw-blonde, practically mute, barely toilet-trained child than he had shown to any of his sons.

What my mother told us about Stephen frightened and confused me even more than stories of Delores. He was my grandmother's last child, hostage to her imbalanced hormones. "Stephen," my mother claimed, "was the one who put your grandmother in her grave." Like Delores, Stephen was retarded, but he had none of the sprightly charm of his sister. He was never able to learn to speak. "He grunted and bullied his way through the family until finally she agreed to put him away in a state hospital," my mother said.

I grew up hearing that Stephen had a child's body, though he was decades older than me. I pictured him trapped in a crib with the side bars pulled up to keep him in his place, out of reach of the other cribs stretching row after row occupied by similar baby adults.

Much to my amazement, my father journeyed once a year, a few weeks before Christmas, to visit his baby brother.

A big cardboard box wrapped in bright Christmas paper by my mother sat on the dining room table. Gradually, it was filled up with things my father bought to bring to Stephen: socks, powder, batteries, bags of sourball candies, red and green candy canes, waxy yellow grapefruits wrapped in tissue paper, large-piece wooden puzzles like the ones I had out grown.

Every day, when he came home from work, my father would put each new item on the dining room table for my mother to wrap.

It made me so angry with him, so jealous. I wasn't jealous of the presents. I was jealous that my father bought each of those items himself, jealous that he made special trips on Saturday mornings to look for particular gifts. Although I was jealous of the smile that that box brought to this dour man's face, I missed that box once it was gone. But I didn't miss my father.

I would come from school on Friday afternoon to find my mother folding his clothes into their brown cardboard suitcase. Later, when my father got home, he was more distracted than usual. He'd carry the Christmas box downstairs and put it on the backseat of the car. My mother placed a basket of food next to him on the front. He'd instruct us to behave and back out of the driveway.

Instantly, the house grew bigger. Chairs, tables, walls and doors, nothing held us back. We were free to be together, to get along, to be silly and laugh and to make our mother laugh. If we fought, and of course we did, it seemed neither urgent nor life threatening. We fought—then forgot about it.

Sometimes I imagined all too vividly those long halls filled with cribs crammed with big infant men, naked, drooling, trying to grab at my father as he walked past, looking for his baby brother, Stephen. I shuddered with the fear that they could pull him back into his own infancy, pull him away from me. My fear startled and confused me, since, in my worst moments, I wished this man dead or at least gone from our lives. Then I would become jealous and angry all over again.

My father returned late on Sunday night, tired but apparently unmoved by the experience (because, of course, he was invulnerable). I seethed with anger and confusion because I felt I had been made a fool by a baby doll uncle who couldn't talk and a father who wouldn't.

***

When our prayers were over, my attention would be wrested finally from the names on that stone and the spirits that haunted it during those visits by the memory of a solemn mission.

Behind me, the only sounds I heard, as I escaped my father's family, were the measured saw of grass clippers and the gritty bite of a spade through dirt. There were none of the usual warnings not to wreck havoc on the world. At the cemetery, the man who claimed our paternity wasn't really present, or he was so intensely "there" that he didn't care if we wandered off.

The breeze alone filled my ears with whispers and welcomes as I ran across the pegged and pillared cemetery like any other boy playing dodge with the dead.

I had another father, a secret father, there in that place of rest, of pause, one I was just as anxious to attend to as my own father was to take care of his. I never thought of this man between visits to the cemetery. In fact, I never remembered him until my father's hand cupped my mother's elbow, lifting her from her prayers onto her tittery high-heeled feet. Then it would be like a tug on my own arm, and I would remember that he was waiting.

His was the only grave site that was cordoned off. A low latticed copper fence, weathered to a sea green, marked the length and width of two plots. Yet it wasn't particularly well tended. The grass looked nibbled instead of cut. Weeds, all gone to seed, entwined with the fence slats.

Inside the enclosure stood a large, seven-foot Byzantine cross, a cross gone crazy with two extra arms, one of which looked as though it had slipped down.

In the center of this towering bluish green copper cross was a picture, encased in plastic, the size and shape of a saucer, of a man. He had a long thin face capped with a thin fringe of hair like a monk's. His shoulders were broad, and a white surplice billowed out like wings. The tab of his clerical collar rose out of the black cassock like a milky jewel. Although he looked acetic and somber, his mouth was soft and full as though the artist (it was a painting, I was to realize years later, not a photograph), or Death, had caught him midsentence. At least that was how I imagined him, always on the brink of telling me something, offering me some word of hope and love.

His eyes, though, had none of that vulnerability or tenderness. They didn't even seem to see me. Those two dots of blackness stared out beyond our family's plot. His gaze just grazed my father's stooped back as he tended to his lost family. The priest looked out over the neighboring steel foundry's endless smelting fires and through the hills that cradled the Hudson. It was the look our history books gave to the brave and intrepid, the look my *Lives of the Saints* gave to the sanctified.

The low gate shivered as I lifted the horseshoe latch and went into the enclosure. Up close like that I could just make out the white and black form; and I knew he couldn't see me. Nevertheless, I felt peculiarly visible, suddenly a boy of flesh and blood, the same boy who most days worked hard to be invisible in that quietly raging place called home. Soon I was pulling up grass from along the fence making sure to throw it outside the grave site. The border never looked as cleared and precise as my father's efforts at the family stone, nor did I seem able to work with his ease or speed. My fingers just as often became entangled in the fence links as they did in the coarse ribbons of crab grass. I was worried my parents would call me back before I was done, so I worked diligently. The grass seemed to grow up behind me as I crept along until finally I gave up and set off to find flowers for this holy man.

I tied a scraggly bouquet together with a rope of grass and lay the flowers at the base of the cross. I inched back to the gate so I could look up into that long, longing face.

I craned my head back so our eyes could meet. His were black, yet beaming with sunlight reflected off his protective dome. Mine were burning, but I didn't dare blink. I was afraid of missing something, a sign, a message.

What I wanted, what I needed, from this solemn saint, was one thing: a word of comfort from beyond the grave that I could give to my father. I was certain this priest knew all the souls of my father's past, of Mary and Dolores and Stephen, of Peter and Euphemia, and of all the other cousins and aunts and uncles who seemed to worry my father when he came to the cemetery and walked that dusty gauntlet of memory. If only this saint could give me a word. Then for once I would be the messenger of good news, a source of comfort, to my father rather than the usual sore of irritation. I knew that if it was going to happen at all it would have to happen here, among these graves. It was only in this narrow parcel of land, on this one day of the year, that my father seemed to have ears that listened, if only to spirit messages. But this time I would be there, and he would notice me and listen to me and take my hand in gratitude.

My eyes began to tear and burn, but still I didn't blink. Just then I was sure that the picture moved. The priest's head bent down toward me. The billowing surpliced wings fluttered. His words were about to form in my ear.

But it was my father's one note whistle that brought me back to earth and to my family like the filament inextricably connecting the spider to its web. It was time to go. My father had his tools in the bushel basket, and Walter was already standing at the gate waiting. Still I couldn't give up. That stoop to my father's usually taut back was too unsettling. So much depended on my being there to get a word for my father. Then his whistle snapped out again. This time it was like the leash that yanks the dog to its master. Desperate with hope, I looked up at the priest. But now I only saw what I had become accustomed to seeing in the eyes of the only father I knew, a glowering, silent stare.

I was the last to get back to the car. Once again, I had let my father down.

The leaden thud of the trunk door told me that my father knew all about my failure. He pulled out onto the road, carefully, because he did everything carefully, and drove away, not looking back, the stunned silent survivor of a deadly accident, completely alone, and completely bereft.

I knew exactly how my father felt.

Our gray Plymouth turned down the soft hills of Watervliet, past the fields of foundry fires, into the Hudson's house-littered valley like a stone rolling to its rest across the entrance to a tomb.

The Widows of Christ's Chapel Assembly of God Church

Susan Sink

Here, the old women
whose healings have worn
to age, mothers, grandmothers

with large losses, free now
to mourn under guise
of worship, to soar

from shapeless puddles
of shoes, from cloy
of old perfume, of salves,

for whom the hymns
are history, the tunes browned
as locket photos

with voices inked by memory,
harmonious bottles of water struck
to wavering, a watery sound

got by heart—what comforts
are the things of this world
still here, words following words,

Sunday mornings
delivered to the doorstep
by kind neighbors, sons, others

who have less need for God,
who hang back, beyond reach
of the hands, the longing

invitation—the Holy
Spirit, tongues breaking
song-prayer to a wail

of want, *hurt*, want
to be whole, healed, to be
held, holy, here.

"Bird in a Tree"
Painting by Keith Abbott

Canto del Amor Perfecto
Carlos Pellicer

Señor,
hoy no te pido nada,
Perfecto es ya mi amor;
sólo dulzura y alabanza
sobre la onda dócil de mi corazón.
Una guirnalda te traigo,
de rosas plateadas y negras;
una lira que sola te canta.
sus brazos son de roble y sus cuerdas,
de palmera.
Te traigo una ola
que salvó toda una noche de pesca.
Las esculturas de los hombres
jamás vieron así a la primavera.
Señor,
tus pies parecen sandalias mágicas.
Tus manos son un poco de agua
con luna,
y de tu gran túnica morada
sale la voz de las albas oscuras.
Tu boca es pálida y serena
como el día que sigue a una batalla.
Tus ojos se abren en la noche
y tu última mirada,
cierra los lentos círculos del alba.
Señor,
tu cuerpo es perfecto
como una dulce ausencia sin nostalgia.
Cuando caminas
bajo los pájaros del estío,
las montanas electrizan
el azul de sus curvas
y la lluvia
cruza
cantando los ríos.
El huracán que rompe sus caracoles,

Song of Perfect Love by Carlos Pellicer
translated by Donny Smith

Lord,
I ask nothing of you today,
already perfect is my love:
only sweetness and praise
on my heart's docile wave.
A wreath I bring you,
of silvered and black roses;
a lyre that sings alone for you,
its arms of oak and its strings
of palm.
I bring you a wave
which I saved one whole night of fishing.
The sculptures of men
not once looked this way at spring.
Lord,
your feet appear to be magic sandals.
Your hands are a little water
with moon,
and from your great purple robe
goes up the voice of dark dawns.
Your mouth is pale and serene
like the day that follows a battle.
Your eyes open in the night
and your last glance,
closes the slow circles of dawn.
Lord,
your body is perfect
like an absence sweet free of longing.
When you walk
under birds of summer,
mountains electrify
the blue of their curves
and rain, singing,
crosses
rivers.
The storm that breaks its shells,

detiene sus ciegas locomotoras
y te tiende una cinta de espumas
sobre el magno poesía de tus olas.
El guardafaro, se vuelve Beethoven
cuando pasas llenándonos con tu vida sinfónica.
Hoy no te pido nada.
Te traigo una guirnalda
de rosas negras y plateadas.
Nada te pido hoy;
sólo te lleno de alabanzas..
Dulzura y albanza; sea perfecto el amor.

halts its blind locomotives
and stretches out a ribbon of foam for you
on the great poem of the waves.
The lighthouse keeper turns into Beethoven
as you pass filling us with your symphonic life.
Today I ask nothing of you.
I bring you a wreath
of black and silvered roses.
I ask nothing today,
only fill you with praises.
Sweetness and praise: may love be perfect.

En Prisión
Carlos Pellicer

¿Qué agua de Ti mi corazón anega?
¿Por qué el viento me empuja hacia la orilla?
Al lago que bajé—noche que brilla—
su ser afín mi corazón entrega.

No senda que pausada en maravilla
a Nínives y a. Uxmales sólo llega.
Es el paisaje de Jesús que entrega
puertas de una ciudad que sin Sol brilla.

Ningún bagaje, ligadura o nudo;
el corazón tan libre y tan desnudo
que lleve las pasiones como estrellas.

Desaparezca la Esperanza y solas
la Fe y la Caridad dejen sus huellas.
Se podrá caminar sobre las olas.

Prisión del Cuartel de San Diego, Tacubaya, febrero de 1930

In Prison by Carlos Pellicer
translated by Donny Smith

What water of You floods my heart?
Why does the wind push me toward the shore?
To the lake I drained—night that shines—
its kindred being hands over my heart.

Not a path that comes in wonder, unhurried,
to Ninevahs and Uxmals only.
It's the landscape of Jesus handing over
the gates of a city that shines without Sun.

No baggage, bond, or knot;
a heart so free and so naked
that it carries passions like stars.

Let Hope disappear, and Faith
and Charity alone leave their print.
One could walk on the waves.

San Diego Barracks Jail, Tacubaya, February 1930

The *Shekhinah*
Davi Walders

"My *Shekhinah* shall go with thee, and give thee rest."
Exod. 33:14 (Onkelos translation)

Before dawn crowns the restless night,
I do not pray exactly, nor hope persuasively,
glancing at cratered eyes of Somali women,
charred hands of a Bosnian child, maps

of shootings, carjackings. I must
work, threading and pulling under
the glare of an October sun, its sullen
splotches spreading across white space

and dark, beseeching, imploring something more
from me. I do not bind the morning's nameless
upon my hands, my gates, nor take them for frontlets
before my eyes. I cannot even name 600 of the 613.

I am a lumberer of alleys and woods, scratching
for spores, rubbing twigs, hunting words to anchor
margins, hungry for the milk of completion,
chilled before winter rejections, seeking,

always seeking ...

until that dusky pause when dust stills
on a deserted desk, the mind's wind chime
quiets in the thickening air, the hesitation
between work and rest, quotidian and holy,

as I watch the wicks spark and flare, my hands
hovering over blue-tipped flames, light arcing.
Margins blend, walls soften, surrendering
to a shadowy caress. This is the call to untie

the heart's tight confusions, to soothe
the week's churning. Ancient sounds
release, rise in an instant's distillation
from the mikvah of souls. Robed in indigo,

they stand silent, swaying, eyes lowered
in prayer. Shadows dance on linen cloth.
Sarah reaching for her child, Rebecca cradling
twins, Rachel's tears dissolving into ruby wine.

Golden challah braided with Miriam's song,
Dinah's whisper. This is the moment beyond memory,
beyond merging, embraced by a presence unfolding.
Morning eyes lighten, bones take on the fullness

of flesh. Wicks bow to melting tallow, petaled
flowers. We are opalescent vessels floating
through gates of this choosing. Warm
arms, sturdy and old, enfold.

This is the solitary, the singular, holding
us, sustaining us, dwelling with us, singing
sweet songs without witness or word, gowning
us in the blessings of light

A Mary

Anya Krugovoy

There's a Mary for everything:
For limestone, for subways, for birches.
There's a Mary for college football,
For the homeless, for abandoned cats
And dogs, for sneaker factories and suburbs.
Everywhere, she casts pitying
Eyes over cathedrals and gardens,
Rear view mirrors and asphalt highways.
And in one small village in Austria,
Maria von dem Schnee, heaped with candles
And evergreen boughs, blesses the snow,
Blesses the skiers, the boot makers, the cows
In their stalls, stomping and breathing white
Plumes through the soundless, snowy evenings.
When, in my narrow bed, sleep won't come,
I think of Maria's placid face, her small hands
Folded, her perpetual benedictions of frosted-
Over car windows and frozen locks,
And my own heart, frigid in its socket
The day I told my lover that I wanted to leave,
Our bed sheets and our hands chapped with cold.
She was my own Mary then, she knew my thoughts
Like a mother, she whispered *Be still, my daughter*
And covered me in her easy snow, blessing
My winter, its deep and early shadows,
The ice beneath my eyelids and the good, good sleep.

before the beginning and after the end
Naomi Ruth Lowinsky

when you wrap me in your shawl
old mother india
and feed me to the rapture of the kites

when the jewels you gave me
are fingered by strangers
and the words i am writing are my flaming
body on the river

will you sweep me up like ash on the wind
and show me all the lives that brought me here?

were those long dark eyes
of a bullock in Orissa—
whose horns are painted yellow and blue
who is adorned with bells and marigolds
and is pulling a plough
after the harvest before the planting of the seed—
ever mine?

or the long arms of the white monkey
wrapped around her baby
on the road to ajanta
whose caves were forgotten
for a thousand years?

or the eyes that were painted
of the mother of buddha
when her son was a dream
that an elephant would pierce her

before the beginning and after the end
will you wrap me up—
old mother—
and feed me to the lives
i've not yet lived?

The Journey Out
Deborah Bacharach

The day I left Egypt the sun
was the same sun I always
carried on my shoulders,
walking bent with the weight.

If a mosquito was whining
or someone moaning, or if
there was the tap, tap, tap
of slow blood dripping down

from a newly slaughtered lamb, I
didn't know it. No angels
singing in my ears, just
the hiss of sand shifting.

When I walked out of Egypt, all
I saw were the heels ahead,
bone dry and cracked, lifting
and falling like a chant.

I smelled salt, my own sweat and something else, the sea faint. It whipped
my eyes to tears, covered
my skin in a white crust.

When we stepped in, you say I looked
the same as when we were slaves.
I felt cool water on my feet,
doubt lapping my heart like a wave.

Listening to *The Berlin Mass* by Arvo Pärt, Performed at Grace Cathedral by the San Francisco Chorus
Gerrye Payne

Deep and still, wide, the well holds water
for the wanderer who turns away
and then returns.

Sweep of stars makes a pattern
we carry with us,
the shape of a wheel, the shape of a jar
that holds what we'll need
tomorrow.

We follow stone steps down,
with our awkward faces
and empty hands,

down to breathe in half-light
far away from the dead-water sellers,

down,
to taste water
that streams from stones.

E-mail to the Lord
Willis Barnstone

I wrote an e-mail to the Lord
who had me in his memory bank
of heretics, marked for his sword
of mercy, and it's true I stank
deep in his nostrils, yet he sent
me back a swift retort, "Don't mess
with heaven, and the years I've lent
you on the earth will stand. But less
than full obedience will earn
you coupons for a room in hell."
To God.org went my reply,
"Lord of the Mountains, will you learn
some manners? Though I know your spell,
kindly bless us on earth, and die."

Standing in Darkness
in a California Hotel Room
Willis Barnstone

> Steve Huff who looks through a wall
> of nothingness to talk with the Buddha

My doctor heals with medicines, although
sometimes the pills don't fix my soul, who hurts
foolishly, fooling me cheerful as snow,
who stuns me up and down. A good word hurts
as much as fear. Was the Buddha serene?
He was a man rocking between hot flesh
and bread and water till he found a lean
midway. He knew the human fire of wish
despair. He was too good not to fear death,
the bug. I stand at three a.m. with him,
poor man, since she my soul is uppity
on this rare night of happiness. The rim
of dark is grinning loose with snow. I'll be
with you, bright soul, dying for each still breath.

The Stolen Saint
Karen Guzman

Larry burst into the kitchen one morning in early autumn, bearing a look of glee that Jerome knew could only mean bad news.

"Hey," Larry said, breathless and wide-eyed, barely able to contain his tittering joy. "Guess what?" The screen door banged shut behind him, shaking the good crystal glasses in the cabinet on the wall. "Guess what? Guess what? Guess what?"

Jerome looked up, spoon paused midway between the bowl of cornflakes on the table and his mouth. "What?"

"Your little buddy Joseph has flown the coop!"

"My ... what are you talking about?"

"Joseph. Saint Joseph, your dumb statue. It's gone!"

"Gone?" Jerome lowered his spoon.

"Kaput, finito, history!" Larry burst into sinister, twelve-year-old laughter and stamped his sneakered feet. "Somebody musta stole the retarded thing!"

Jerome sighed. He was losing the battle this morning to keep his irritation with Larry in check.

"Kidnapped!" Larry said. "And the funniest part is—who would want it, Jerome, besides you?"

Jerome pointed his spoon at Larry. "Listen, if you hid that statue or buried it or something, you're going to be VERY sorry."

"Yeah? Why? Is Joseph gonna get me? Gonna strike out at me from the other side?"

Jerome shook his head. The wave of irritation swelled. Ordinarily he was better at ignoring Larry's obnoxious comments, at letting them roll off his back. But not lately.

"What normal person keeps a ratty, paint-peeling saint in the backyard anyway?"

"Just mind your own business," Jerome mumbled. "Brat."

"Jerk-off."

"Larry!" their mother broke in, turning from the sputtering hiss of the coffee machine on the counter. "What did I tell you about that language?"

"Sorry, I forgot."

Jerome knew that Larry had only recently learned what "jerk-off" meant. Kenny Clemens at school had told him. Clemens' older brother had secret copies of *Playboy* and *Hustler*. Jerk-off was the single, most hilarious word Larry had ever heard. Jerome wasn't surprised. The start of a new school year always brought out the worst in the little twerp. Only this time, Jerome had no patience for it. This was his senior year at Glen Run High School, and there were bigger things looming.

He pushed his chair back from the kitchen table. "I'll be right back."

"You'll be late for school," his mother said.

"This'll just take a sec." He glanced at Larry. "I'm not giving you a ride. You can take your bus." He had a license and his own car, a used Dodge his father had helped him rebuild. The Dodge was olive green, but the driver and passenger doors they'd salvaged from the junk yard were red. Jerome had never got around to repainting them. Larry said the car looked like something a serial killer would drive cross-country.

"Like I really want a ride from you," Larry said now and grinned, drawing his lips back in the ferocious little sneer Jerome hated.

Jerome snorted, grabbed the screen door handle and stepped out into the sunshine.

In mid-September, the days were ripe and lingering, the mornings stirring with the first cool undercurrents of autumn. He walked briskly over a lawn still green and hopeful, though touches of yellow spotted the tree branches. The trees lining the road, too, were splashed with ruby and gold. The trees in autumn were one of the first things that had made him believe in God. All his life he'd had a series of touchstones, little links to God, he could reach for. Only somehow over the years, they'd grown fewer and harder to recall. And when he did reach for them now—now, just as he was contemplating a life in the church—he was often alarmed to find they had lost their magic.

Larry was right; Joseph was gone. A circle of bare, brown soil marked the spot, like a bruise, at the edge of the brook where the statue had stood for years. How many years? At least ten. It was only Saturday that he had last checked on Joseph. Over the years it had become a habit—his Saturday walks to the backyard, where he would bend and touch the statue's cool head. Always it made him feel better. Anchored. Reconnected to a God who peered into his heart and understood all things. He squatted now and pressed his palm against the cool earth. Staring at the soil, he felt as if a piece of his own body—some silent, essential organ deep within—had been extracted and carried off. A sharp pain pierced beneath his breastbone, and he sensed he was alone as he had never been before.

He had won Joseph in the county carnival when he was nine. He'd tossed three rubber rings around a peg and been offered his choice of the prizes on the shelves behind the carnival man with the spooky glass eye. The whole family had gone to the carnival that night. Larry was only four and afraid of the rides. Jerome had become separated from his parents and wandered to the ring game booth alone. The carnival man urged him to hurry and pick a prize. People were waiting. He spotted the statue, in between the cap guns and plastic dinosaurs. Something in Joseph's delicately stenciled blue eyes, gazing out at the carnival with calm tolerance, called to him. Even at nine, he'd realized the guy in the statue must have known something big, something really worth knowing. When he showed his parents, his father laughed and his mother said the statue would look nice in the backyard. On the way home in the car, he carried Joseph on his lap, the plaster cool beneath his hands. He was charmed, but something in his father's laughter— a mocking undercurrent that would always be there—pricked at him. Still, Joseph and he shared a silent alliance, a secret collusion that was impervious to the outside world. Joseph was a sweet-faced sentinel at the edge of the lawn, holding back the dark woods.

"Jerome?" his mother called from the back door. "Honey, you'll be late."

"I'm coming." He turned and headed quickly across the yard. The screen door banged shut behind him. His mother stood in the middle of the kitchen, her lips drawn in an unspoken question.

"It's gone," he said, turning quickly away.

Upstairs before the bathroom mirror, he ran a comb through his short, dark hair. His hair wasn't black like his mother's or a wheat-colored blond like his father's. It was a rich chestnut hue, thick and wavy. He kept it cut short. Too short, his mother complained, for such beautiful hair. His eyes matched his hair. He had fine, regular features and was at last starting to fill out. He was nearly five-foot-eleven and had been skinny far too long.

He began brushing his teeth, then heard Larry yelling in the backyard. He went to the bedroom window and saw Larry, hands cupped around his mouth.

"Jerome, hey Jerome?" Larry called. "Look at it this way. Maybe someone did us a favor, and hauled Joseph's peeling, plaster ass down to the dump!"

***

Long after the television news ended that night and his father's footsteps had faded down the hall, Jerome lay awake, as he often did. It was astounding, he had realized that summer, how round the moon was, how it hung in the sky, a perfect, smooth sphere. And the light, the ghostly glow that lit the backyard, sparking off the glassy surface of the brook at the edge of the lawn. When Larry and he were younger, they'd played a game called "Follow the Watery Way." The winner was the one who dared to follow the brook farthest, way back into the woods where you couldn't see anything and the tree branches seemed to shimmer with secret life. It had been a great game at sleepovers when a bunch of guys pitched pup tents, his mother brought out plates of brownies and cookies, and everyone made a racket, shrieking and running around until his father called from an upstairs window, "Hey fellas, think it's time you give it a rest now?"

Jerome always won "Follow the Watery Way." Always. Because back then, he'd been fearless. This fear had begun later, and grown with time. It was always there now, this vague uneasiness, the suspicion that he had been wrong about so many things. That he was wrong now—deluded maybe—believing God was calling him. There was no way of knowing.

Up close the moon probably wasn't that round. There were probably a number of explanations. Distance and perspective, the blurring of the two. That's the type of thing his father would point out. His father was a chemist. He worked in research at one of the big pharmaceutical companies, making medicines that saved people's lives. Jerome was proud of him, though it wasn't the type of thing he'd say to his face. He sometimes asked God to deliver the message and thought he felt God reply: Tell him yourself.

***

The letter arrived a week later. He came home from school and found the envelope, plain white, addressed to him in scrawling black ink, sitting on the kitchen counter. The postmark was Jersey City, New Jersey, a good hour away. Jersey City was a place he'd seen on the news: fires, drug arrests, shootings. He didn't know anyone from Jersey City. He tore open the envelope and drew out a single snapshot, a three-by-four inch glossy. No note or letter. Just the picture. It was in color—rows of seats, a line of people standing before some sort of counter. A waiting room? In the upper right hand corner, a white sign: "Departing Flights." An airport. He frowned. Who would send him a picture of an airport terminal? Then he saw Joseph. There, propped alone on one of the seats in the middle of an empty row. He almost didn't recognize the statue at first. The photograph wasn't centered. Joseph was off to the side, almost as if the photographer hadn't been focusing on him.

Still it was undeniably Joseph, looking small, forgotten, and absurdly out of place. The pointy, serene face stared straight ahead. Tall glass windows loomed in the background. When Jerome squinted, he could make out the faint figure of a plane in the gray beyond the glass. He flipped the photo over. On the bottom, in swirly, round handwriting: "Dearest Jerome, I'm off! So much to see, so little time! Wish you could come—but, hey, you're in my thoughts. Besides I wouldn't want you bringing me down. Love always, Joe."

The breath trailed from his body, as if someone had delivered a powerful, slow-motion punch to his gut. He turned to the window, to the endless silent sky, and asked why. And nothing happened.

***

"I swear to holy God Almighty, you hear that Jerome? God Almighty, I said, that I had nothing to do with Joseph getting to the airport." Larry wasn't even smiling as he said this. He'd already smiled. He'd collapsed with giggles and rolled on the living room rug, gasping after he saw the picture.

"Liar," Jerome replied flatly, not so much because he believed Larry was lying, but because, huddled in his father's study, he could think of nothing else to say.

His father squinted at the picture, holding it under the desk lamp. He'd already deduced that the airport must have been Newark International. Given the Jersey City postmark, it made sense.

Behind gold wire eyeglasses, his father wore a bland expression, but Jerome suspected he was secretly celebrating. Although his father had always tolerated his beliefs—fainty amused, biting his tongue sometimes—he had drawn the line at college. His father had been against this "Bible college thing" from the start. What had he called it? A colossal, staggering waste of a mind. That was back at the beginning of the summer, when they were really going at it. Now his father had gone underground, silently searching for an opening, anything to turn Jerome against Northeastern Bible College. Or Holy Roller U, as he called it.

His father turned to him, and Jerome felt the room close in. "This is just a stupid gag," his father said. "It's nothing to get ... worked up about. Don't let it distract you, Jerome, in the middle of your college applications. They're a lot more important than an old statue."

Jerome shrugged, desperate to cover his mounting panic. In the dark-paneled, scholarly study, he was more exposed than ever. The walls, lined with diplomas and citations—his father was a Princeton man— seemed only to amplify his own foolishness. The dignified leather spines of the encyclopedias, the scientific journals, silent and smug in their knowledge. His father was right. He'd always been right.

"So he's left the state," Larry said, hovering between Jerome and their father, eyes bright with drama.

"What?" his father said.

"Joseph. He must have left the state. Maybe someone kidnapped him, tied him up, gagged him, hustled him off in the middle of the night."

His father stood and snapped off the desk lamp.

"He coulda easily gotten on that plane," Larry continued.

"Let it go," his father said. "Dinner's almost ready."

Jerome turned away from the accusing book shelves, but Larry went on. "Anyone coulda smuggled Joseph on board. Even as carry-on luggage, right? You wouldn't have to check him. Just stick him in the overhead storage bin above your seat."

"Larry, let it... "

"Just stick him in the bin, and listen to him rattle around during takeoff."

"Are you deaf, Larry?" Jerome said. "Drop it already."

But Larry's dark eyes were far away, conjuring, preparing for one of his startling leaps in logic. "Listen, you gotta admit: He'd fit in the overhead storage bin," he insisted.

Their father sighed and headed for the door. Jerome followed, then hesitated, turning back to Larry. "Yeah, so what?" he asked. "So what if he'd fit in the overhead bin?"

"That's all," Larry said lightly. "That's all I'm saying. He'd fit. The statue would fit. It's a small thing, Jerome. A small thing."

His father spun back around. "Oh, Jerome, about your applications. I thought I could maybe go through them with you? Read over the essay questions, take a look at what you write?"

Jerome's heart thudded two hard beats. His breath caught for a second. "Sure," he said. "Sure, Dad. I'll ... I'll let you know when they come."

"Hey, why don't we call the cops?" Larry asked suddenly. "About Joseph? Report it missing or ... or stolen? The stolen saint?"

Jerome wheeled around but then stopped. Larry's dark eyes were wide and round, his smooth face open. A smudge of chocolate pudding stained one corner of his mouth. He blinked. There was no hint of mockery in his simple suggestion. He looked for an instant the way he had on those dark nights in the backyard. Little Larry, standing at the edge of the woods with a flashlight, his mouth gaping, watching his big brother disappear. And something caught in the back of Jerome's throat. "Maybe I will," he said. He couldn't say any more, for he was back in the woods, under the stars, with the confident shrieks, the unthinking bravado, of little boys all around. And fixed in the dark sky above them was a moon forever round and perfect and knowing.

***

The college applications sat on a pile on his desk. There were five: Rutgers, the state university, big and sprawling, you could major in anything you wanted there; Michigan State; the University of Pennsylvania; Wesleyan, with its Methodist roots; and ... Northeastern Bible College. *Holy Roller U.*

Maybe his father was right. He'd go to a *real* college, submerge himself, put the pastor thing on hold. He'd make sure first. This was surely a fine plan, a reasonable plan. Why then was he unable to act? He prayed fervently, but nothing was any clearer. The applications taunted him. He'd sit at his desk and stare at them, the questions and orderly little boxes awaiting his responses.

***

A week later, the second letter arrived. This one contained a photograph of Joseph on a bar stool. The lights were dimmed. A hint of hazy smoke hung in the air. Rows of bottles glinted above a cash register, next to a neon Budweiser sign in the shape of a guitar. Someone had placed a full martini glass, the green olive suspended inside, on the wooden bar before Joseph. The note on the back: "I'm tossing one back for you, kid. Love always, Joe."

Someone, somewhere was certainly having a good time. Some sicko. Jerome tried to cut a deal with God. Please, can this just stop? I'm lost and screwed-up, I know, but if this can just stop, maybe we can work out the rest. He prayed with no feeling of certainty that he'd be answered. Certainty belonged to the past. His entire life had been a fraud. He had no idea what to do next. And he still had to ask Helen Ditmars to the prom. He had cornered her two or three times at their lockers already, trying to get the words out. I was wondering if maybe you, ah, had a date to the prom yet? And if you don't, I was wondering if you, ah, maybe wanna go with me? He'd liked her since eighth grade. He either had to make his move now or give it up. She'd applied for early acceptance to Smith College. No Bible schools for Helen. Not that it mattered. For eyes like hers, and those tight wool skirts that fell over her hips in soft waves, he could make exceptions. Maybe he could make one for college, too. Maybe things had never been what he'd imagined. He felt his own heart beating and the hollow rush of air moving in and out of his lungs. He felt everything, and no one knew.

One night, sitting before the applications on his desk, he blurted it out—the real truth—to, of all people, Larry.

Larry had an uncanny knack for showing up during Jerome's moments of crisis, and could at times be extremely sensitive to atmosphere. He was passing in the hall, on the way to his own bedroom, when he spotted Jerome, sitting motionless, and stopped in the doorway of his brother's room. "Hey, the Nets won," Larry said.

Jerome turned to the door. "I'm alone. We're all alone," he said. "I've been such a fool all this time. Such an idiot. It's all been just a big joke, hasn't it?"

Larry paused, confused. "What's a joke?"

Jerome felt the stupid, hot tears fill his eyes. He turned his back to Larry.

"Hey Jerome?" Larry said quietly.

He didn't answer. What was the point?

"Hey Jerome? Hey jerk-off?" Larry practically whispered.

"Go to bed," he said wearily.

"Hey, listen, Jerome. Just listen: No one's laughing."

***

As soon as he pulled open the mailbox and saw the white envelope inside, he knew what it was. He didn't even stop to read the address. Joseph. This time standing, dwarfed in the arched threshold of some sort of theater. A crowded street before him, faceless strangers passing on the sidewalk. And the marquee above his head declaring in bright red, block letters: Passion Palace. All Girls, All Nude, All The Time. Jerome blinked, turned the photograph over. "A night to remember. You should have been with us, big guy. It would have rocked your world. Love always, Joe."

Jerome went numb. He stuffed the picture back in the envelope. This one he wasn't showing to his father or to Larry. Larry'd go crazy. He walked slowly back up the road and found his mother in the yard, watering her mums. They were the last surviving flowers, growing alone in the hard soil along the house.

"Another one," he said, handing her the envelope.

Her eyes widened. She dropped the hose and pulled the picture from the envelope. One hand rose to cover her astonished, open mouth. "Looks like Times Square," she said. She was silent a moment; then she cracked a smile. "I'm sorry, Jerome. I am. It's just ... " She bit her lip. "So ridiculous," she said, erupting into laughter.

He was angry at first and then surprised to feel her laughter move over him in a warm wave. Something in the gardening gloves she clasped in one hand, in the sputtering drip of the hose at her feet, and the first shadows of the evening gathering at the edge of the lawn, reached out to him, told him the world was still here and would continue to revolve on schedule. This much, these simple things, he could be certain of.

"I'm not showing Dad this one," he said. "Or Larry either."

"Oh no. God forbid, Larry," his mother said, wiping her eyes. The mums shimmered. Droplets fell from their bright petals, orange and yellow and gold, down into the dark soil.

***

The next day he asked Helen to the prom. If Joseph could visit a girlie bar, he could at least muster the courage to ask someone for a date. And the astonishing thing was, Helen said yes. She said yes in the most casual way, smiling before their lockers, as if she'd been waiting for him to get around to it. As if she were wondering what the big deal was. Then she went to class. As easy as that.

He wandered into chemistry, took his usual seat. Since eighth grade, he had schemed and deliberated. He had debated and rehearsed. And she said yes. Sure. Slammed her locker door and strolled off. He sat back in his seat. Was he the only one who made such a big to-do, such a fuss, about things? Enough was enough. He wanted answers. He wanted in on the big secret, whatever it was that everyone else seemed to know. Larry watched the Nets win, rejoiced, and fell asleep. His father lapsed into a satisfied silence when Jerome agreed to let him read over the college essay questions. His mother faithfully watered her mums, happy to keep them alive into the cold days and nights as long as possible. They took comfort wherever it could be found. Could it really be that simple?

After class he prayed for a sign, alone in the boys' bathroom. Standing before the row of porcelain sinks and mirrors, he closed his eyes and concentrated, attuning his body to any flicker of reassurance. He waited. The tap dripped. Someone passing in the hall outside laughed. He opened his eyes to his own pale, uncertain face in the mirror.

***

In the next photograph, Joseph is standing alone in the center of a long, flat stretch of empty highway. He is perhaps in the desert. Yes, in the distance, where the highway arches slightly upward, you can see the hazy blur of heat rising from the asphalt. You can almost feel the arid air, the gritty scrape of sand on pavement, the clouds of hot, choking dust that rise when a lone car speeds by.

Joseph is either lost or abandoned. It's difficult to say which. Maybe both. He is dwarfed by the hint of a vast landscape all around him. The desert, perhaps the Grand Canyon. He is in the middle of nowhere, with no discernible way of getting out. Yet he appears unfazed, stalwart, his white robe falling in the same plaster folds it always has. His straight, unflinching posture and peaceful gaze. There is this utter acceptance Joseph possesses. Not defeat, you understand. But acceptance. There's a difference. This is what has always stirred beneath the sky-blue eyes with their white pinpoints of light. It's what Jerome recognized but could not name or even grasp at the carnival all those years ago.

On the back of this photograph, a short note: "We all end up here eventually, Buddy. Love always, Joe."

And Jerome thinks, Yes, we do.

Of course there was no such photograph. Jerome dreamed this one. He woke in the dark silence of his bedroom, with the heat of the highway all around, the dust and longing etched into his skin. And he knew they would always be there.

***

That weekend, he filled in the applications. Once he got started, his pen flew over the pages. He'd already told the high school to send his transcripts on to the colleges he'd selected. Including Northeastern Bible College. At the desk in his bedroom, he wrote two essays. In one, he emphasized his accomplishments, his stellar grades and test scores, the proof every college prized. But in the other—the one he sent only to Northeastern Bible College—he put everything: the night at the carnival, the pup tents in the backyard, seven-year-old Larry standing at the edge of the woods, the rich red of the center aisle carpet in church, the gleaming wooden pews, Helen's easy smile, his father's encyclopedias, and most of all how Joseph had disappeared from the spot where the trees grew dense and the way uncertain, and still he had gone on.

His father cleared his throat after reading the essays. "They're very good, very ... better than I expected," he said. Then he held up the Bible college essay. "Especially this one," he said. "I see you feel, ah, quite strongly about this, Jerome, maybe more strongly than I'd realized." He placed the essays down on the desk. "Let's just wait now and see what happens, see where you get accepted. I'm sure something can be worked out," he said. Then he nodded reassuringly and turned away.

But Jerome had heard the unspoken words. He had seen the glimmer, the relief, in his father's eye. All words that were too difficult to speak aloud, too laden with love and the fear of failure and reprisal—all these were here only on Jerome's behalf. And if Joseph had taught him anything, it was not to miss these signs that sometimes pass between people.

***

He woke Monday morning early, and lying in the pearly gray dawn of his bedroom, sensed a new chill in the air. The first cold morning of autumn. There would be a stiff frost on the lawn. He wanted to see it.

In sweat pants and a t-shirt, shivering slightly, he crossed his room, bare feet moving across the cold carpet into the hall, onto the smooth, wooden floorboards. He passed Larry's room, the sight of comic books and sneakers strewn across the floor and Larry, a small, still lump beneath a blanket. The door to his parents' room at the end of the hall was closed. Downstairs he moved through the dim living room, past the couch and the coffee table on whose corner Larry had once split a lip, past the piano covered with family photographs in glinting silver frames.

In the kitchen, the light grew stronger, flooding the windows over the sink. Outside, a damp, new day took hold. He cracked open the back door, pulled the screen door behind it, and stepped out onto the top cement step. The cold air was exhilarating. It sharpened his senses, quickened his blood. Frost glittered like a handful of tiny gems thrown across the lawn. In the trees above, a kaleidoscope of dying leaves shimmered, a few letting go to float zigzag to the ground. He breathed deeply and glanced down. On the step below stood Joseph. Jerome let out a shocked cry and dropped to his knees. He trembled in disbelief, grasping this recovered piece of himself. Joseph was smooth and solid and heavy in his hands. It was unbelievable. He closed his eyes and couldn't open them again, for fear the statue would disappear or turn into something else, some similar object he had mistaken in the early morning light. He bowed his head. My God, my God, can this be true?

When at last he did look again, he saw that it was Joseph, only the statue wasn't the same. He turned the figure over, inspecting it for any sign, any clue as to what had happened. There was a small chip on Joseph's left arm, a tiny nick in the folds of the white robe. The round pedestal on which the saint stood was battered, more scuffed than Jerome had remembered. The flesh-colored paint of the hands and face was washed-out. New damage or had this happened before, during all the years in the snow and rain and sun, when he wasn't paying attention? It was hard to tell.

Only Joseph's eyes were the same. A bit of their freshness gone, the points of light perhaps dulled. It was the expression that hadn't changed, the encompassing look of wonder and pity and recognition—all at the same time. An embrace of such fullness, such complete inclusion, that Jerome knew Joseph no longer belonged at the edge of the woods. He lifted the lifeless plaster, held it closer, and brought it inside.

What Is Sacred
Virgil Suárez

When the crow in luminous blue/black
feather comes to offer the last rites

& all the white noises stop—fade
into an eternity of chatter, you

will close your eyes to the world & rest.
Those of us left here will wonder what language

is this left us. What signs & symbols.
We will speak in forked tongues.

We will wait for the crow to spread
its wings and vanish, taking with it

all understanding, all breath.
In this limbo of the exile,

                  this is how belief ends.

Swallows
Karla Van Vliet

Sliding through the seemingly empty air,
their winged shadows flicker
over the sky-stained field pond.
I am driving my girl to sleep
but the moment I see them,
the twenty or thirty dashing
black bodies, there is
something more to this drive
than her nodding head
in the rearview mirror.
Some space that
opens within me—a field,
damp-aired and cool.
I shelter the acreage
with the rounded
fence of my ribs.
There, the clouds move,
straying their wet bodies
over spring plowing,
the edging of bud-tipped trees.

Difficulty
Ailish Hopper

I turned a page,
and there you lay. A word
in a language
that no one says.

And you'd been applied
by a generous brush, just

dipped
in the richest of inks.
Something must have
relented,

and slowly spread
you across
this brilliant field,

in the color
of night,
in shapes like breath,

to teach me: darkness
is not lack
      of light.

For a guided meditation
Valerie Robles

For a guided meditation:

     Breathe in, out
Over a field of sun-scarlet begonias—
          Sweet harmonious chimes
     of Indian Camel Bells
        salty ocean mist
     in the mouth and eyes,
          pursed lips, a paper cut on my right index finger;
     the light channeled
        through the bright vowels of this day,
           this hour
           my minute.

The tiny lifelines on my hands
        like a second rate travel narrative,
        where I've spent the night in jail in Havasu
           barefoot and barely drunk
             like Thoreau,
           knowing only, that I took a stand,
               seeing for the first time
          the true stars above Arizona
             waiting for no one.

     No concern for where I'm going—
          the lines are the limit,
     following left to right
        little severed branches
          straying from their path.
And I wonder,
     Is one of those, today?

     I focus on the simple project of my breath
        in and out
        out and in—
I don't look beyond my arms, extended,

chapped skin
overgrown cuticles,
mid-digital hair.
Staring into my right palm
Joshua speaks to me—
"I've never seen lines like these!"
And I wonder,
what makes my lines, my life,
different?
Even significant, perhaps
as one star among the lake of stars
its lost light years coming down to me—
the stillness of my energy
is as it should be
in this blue moment, in midnight, on this half of the earth
the Loveliness
of all that is
flows through the circle
of breath

So, I breathe.

Practice
Julie Jordan Hanson

And I remembered to be still again
and was given this: a speck dropping
through the air of the adjoining room
had stopped, and was now identifiably
a spider gliding down as segments of its one
filament were spun, pausing in production,
then riding down along the newly-done.

This brought on a long, long chain
of practicing wave-hands-like-clouds
(imagining, in alternation, fog,
horizon, fog…) around the dining table
and past the easy chairs and at the walls reversing
easily like breathing and forgetting.
And as I moved through the rooms,

the air was soft and cool; the hour of rain
was in it and the lilies of the valley that have come
thick by the walk and thick by the ivy.
I stayed outside of thinking. Only two
abrupt exceptions: the brighter green at the tips
of the spruce and cedar, and how the spider
had lowered in segments of its making.

Śavāsana (The Corpse Pose)
Rebecca Morgan Frank

a roomful of corpses Stillness more like naptime   their bones spread before me
softened by the rise and fall of breath I hover Angel Mother Guardian my voice
the bridge between here and there liminal world resting between waking and dreaming
all ages of bones beating hearts laying before me   Once they moved like puppets my
voice the string the loneliness of one voice my voice washing across these bare hearts
before me built on bones these softened faces will go sleep in their own homes trying to
remember the space between my words the place where they come looking for God or
peace or flexibility or maybe just a good nap these bodies these bones these beating hearts
resting in the quiet of my voice   waiting to be called back to the living

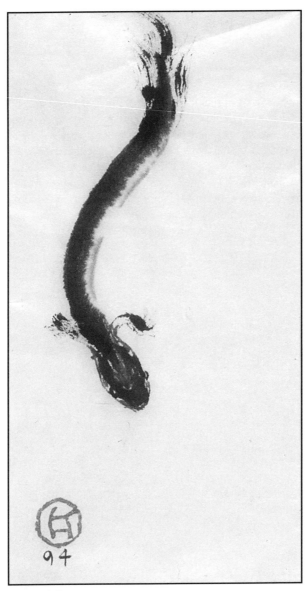

"Tadpole"
Painting by Keith Abbott

Tikkun*
Adrienne Ross

(*To mend, repair, transform—Hebrew)

At Squire Creek, I find a pink salmon stranded on the edge of a pool. He has the look of a pugilist battling unfavorable odds. A dark, squat body. Fanged, distended jaws. September and October bring the smell of the coming winter in the quick, dark rains. Fall brings the Jewish High Holy Day of Yom Kippur—the Day of Remembrance—and halting prayers for my father's memory. It brings pink and other salmon species returning home to spawn and die in their natal creeks. Fungus gold as an ancient coin tinges the pink's humped back. Jaws pump *open shut open shut* pushing sand and iridescent water over his gills. (*You have nothing to do but live*, writes poet Jody Aliesan.)

Sunlight dazzles between rainstorms. Somewhere downstream Squire Creek forked into a thin spur dead-ending in rock and shifting sand bars. Uprooted, wind-worn trees lie scattered like I-Ching sticks. A sharp sweet smell of ripeness gone too far fills the air. Salmon carcasses lie belly up. Their twisted bodies bubble with pink algae. Their slack jaws gape with bronze maple leaves. In the pool dying pinks circle beneath a slow, swirling mosaic of gold conifer needles, amber cedar fronds, bits of ebony-edged bone lichen.

I feel as alert and peaceful in the morning's silence.

I last saw pink salmon two winters ago. In the coastal streams of Asia and North America that still have salmon, one run of pinks will spawn in an even numbered year, while a second, genetically distinct run spawns in odd numbered years. Washington State's pinks spawn in odd numbered years, and so it was in 1997 that I saw my first pink as Squire Creek shimmered past red cedars. RVs were rumbling into the streamside campground. I could hear a steady pounding of traffic down Highway 530 echoing past horse pastures and espresso huts.

I had stood shivering in that distant winter day's thin rain slowly realizing that what I had thought were stones and twists of current were instead pink salmon holding still in the fast water. Their white underbellies blended with the mottled stones beneath them. Three, four, a dozen were nearly hidden in the dull, shifting light reflecting off the creek. The males' humps were an elusive clue to their presence.

The pink twitching at my feet two years later is what remains of that winter run. I lean back against an uprooted tree and watch the pink. Gold and silver motes swirl in crepuscular rays above the dying fish. He lies flat against the stones and clear water. His olive-grey, speckled tail jerks up. He lies still again. His hooked jaws push short, slight ripples of shimmering water over his gills.

Brief weeks ago the pink was sleek, silvery as he traversed the North Pacific and Puget Sound. Following the age-old cycle, once in fresh water the pink stopped eating. His muscles softened. His skin thickened and body darkened. Hooked jaws and the male's characteristic hump formed. His gonads matured for mating, his digestive organs atrophied, and he began feeding off his own body reserves. He has not eaten for weeks. He is one of the lucky ones. Pinks are the most abundant of salmon species, but upwards of an estimated 95% fall prey to fishing fleets and the waiting jaws of a vast ocean. This late in his short, two-year life there are only two things left to do: mate in the same stretch of creek where he was born, and die. A slow weakening and a fast current must have pushed him from the deep water into this meandering trickle. Here the creek has cut its bank. Pale, rain soft bodies of pinks and chinook float tangled in the dirt-flecked roots of alder, cedar, fir.

The pink's tail heaves. Smack. The fish is still. Another heave. Smack. Smack. His soft belly is now firm against the gravel. His dark, fungus-mottled body towers above the clear water. He jerks his tail back and forth, back and forth. He swims forward. The trickle of creek ends in gritty sand and broken twigs. He falls back on his side. He lies still save for the slow pumping of jaws.

I was raised to be afraid of death. The end of life. The void. My father's month of belly tubes, dripping IVs, whispers, silences. (*Dying is a wild Night and a new Road*—Emily Dickinson.) The pink's death is not the death I was taught to fear. It is not death at all if death means finality, cessation, rupture. In their death salmon are the great gift of life.

If I come back in a day or a week, I will find fins, grey flesh, bone, nitrogen, the distant ocean between the tight curls of sword fern fronds, mossy rocks, gnarled umber roots. The Pacific salmon's return, death and eventual decay restore nutrients that have drained off the land and flowed out to sea with the incessant winter rains. Plankton eat these nitrates, phosphates, and other nutrients only to be eaten in turn by larger organisms. Eventually these once land-locked nutrients travel through the ocean's food chain and return to Squire Creek's remaining forests as pink salmon, their eye sockets picked clean, their twisted skeletons cloaked by fallen alder leaves as if ready to swim out of the moist earth and back to the river. (*The great essence will flower in our lives and expand throughout the world*, reads a modern version of the Kaddish, the Jewish prayer for the dead. *We praise, we continue to praise, and yet whatever it is we praise is quite beyond the grasp of all these words*.)

Eagles, shrews, and coyotes feed on the salmon's return. Black tailed deer nibble the stream-side carcasses. Grizzly bears will carry salmon—and the nitrogen, selenium, and iron vitally needed by native flora—as far as a mile from spawning sites. Among the dozens of creatures attending the feast are the aquatic insects that in turn will be eaten by next season's salmon fry.

The exchange of flesh and fin. The bits of bone now scattered between stones. Through it all body, flesh, matter decomposes to its elemental forms: carbon, iron, oxygen, and the other atoms of life that go on merging, combining, creating new structures. Four billion or so years ago adenine, thymine, cytosine, and guanine merged and replicated to become DNA. Now upwards of one and half million to perhaps thirty million species exist on Earth including the genus *oncorhynchus*—Pacific salmon—which took up permanent residence in the Pacific Northwest some 10,000 years ago with the last retreat of the glaciers.

In the Kabbalah, the Jewish mystical tradition, G-d's essence was believed to be contained in holy vessels which broke upon arriving in this earthly realm, scattering and hiding sparks of divine, generative light amid flesh, bone, stone. *Every day the glory is ready to emerge from its debasement*, writes Rabbi Nachman, the mystic of Bratslav. My father was a devout man. His brief joys, brittle dreams, and long life of illnesses stand between me and an abiding trust in G-d. If G-d promises no succor, I have come to find grace in creation. Death is our realm's old, worn coin. Waiting to emerge from its humbling, perhaps debasing exchange is life.

My breath. My father's breath. A desiccated white moth twists in the broken strands of a spider's web. The pink's gills continue their slow, slight pumping. The tail slaps faintly. *You have nothing to do but live* because life is inevitable, inexhaustible, and death is simply life in another form.

Five years of September, October, November, December watching pinks, chinooks, coho, sockeye, chum salmon fully alive as they die. I am no longer afraid to be near death. I was frightened fourteen years ago in my father's narrow, white-walled hospital room. Our decision to curtail life support embarked my father on a new road under a wild, week-long night of the stone clutch of paralyzed muscles, the whispered begging for ice chips to ease starvation. His bones became ashes that became the earth between the roots of an orange tree, became stone, feather, fin, the dark fleck of an eye.

Wind pours through moss-draped alders. Cedar boughs sway in its wake. Creaks turn to a snap. A thin branch of lichen dappled alder falls on the sandbar. I use it to gently push the pink into deeper water. Death will come soon enough. Eros' inevitable shadow or the tearing paws of a raccoon. The pink slips through the murky water. He snaps weakly before settling beside another male.

Somewhere the eggs of the pink's offspring pulse in shadowed, cold water that pours like wind amidst blunt gravel. Faith incarnate. In January, in April, in May the eggs will hatch. The alevin will stay sheltered in the gravel feeding off their swollen yolk sacs. One night they will emerge as silvery, green-backed fry swimming into Squire Creek's flow. They will stay only long enough to imprint on the stream's distinct mineral scent before heading quickly downstream to estuaries. Some Washington pink stocks will journey up the coasts of British Columbia and Alaska following innate magnetic maps of the world. Others will stay in Puget Sound. The survivors will heed their eerie genetic call to return home. To mate and die in the place you were born. A perfect circle in an imperfect world.

"Toad"
Painting by Keith Abbott

Mystic Mountain
(Long Valley, New Jersey)
Dorothy Ryan

Folding clothes in the dark
so the dogs don't see me
and bark to be let in,
I wonder how I came
to be standing
in this space
when my mind is still
in the kitchen
of our old house, where
just last week I stood
folding sheets in the dark
so the dogs wouldn't see me
and bark to be let in.

I long to be back in the old
laundry room, staring
at familiar shadows,
listening to the hum
of the ancient Maytag.
Here, the moon rises high
over the mountain. The wind
whips up from the meadow,
whirls around my legs. My body
floats like swirling leaves.

Am I in or am I out?

The dogs would tell me
if they could.
They would say
the moon is as high
here as it was there.
The stars are as bright.
Be with the fold.
Smooth with your hands.
Let the softness of fabric
ground you to your space,

this place, this dark
enveloping you,
stars climbing
the midnight sky
like an inlaid pattern
in the galaxy.

Drifting from the Moon
Jack Vian

My Buddha stands above
Tears in his eyes
Smoke in his eyes
Steel reflecting in the water
Of his holy belly glittering
Like the reflections of mine
Where teardrop Christs
Spread their glowing wings
Their gentle wood and iron
Tatterdemalion wings.

This Time
Robert Manaster

You will surely wear yourself out, and these people as well ...
—Exodus 18:18

Even now, you must save yourself from a slew of the weary,
A turning away from the too bright, from glints
Of a vessel too strewn to hold any relation to itself;
And you must save all hands losing their light, last reach,
Save dying fragments of song: Somehow, your voice must release those free
In heart from unjust gain and war,
Those who know and love truths, those who judge
By neither trawling all movement in the sea
Nor by letting the light, last seed
Fall into a trough of wind. Your ancient voice must release
Those firm in judgment who know what it is to be
In awe and fear of godliness while being untouched
By feelings of self-immensity. You must release ones
Who can listen well to language beyond the borders
Of iron words and fists. Yes—God be willing—
You must reveal once more how to get it done.
This time you must give us the strength to choose:
Perhaps this time in this age we'll get it right,
This time you as well as God can rest.

Diasporo
Felicia Mitchell

You can't find your own way home again.
The clay that shaped your body
will have been washed away in a flood,
and your blood will be so full of water
that it pales when it spills from your broken heart
like dew or half-hearted tears.
You are here now, right here:
the ground beneath your tired feet concrete.
Inside your shoes, your feet may remember another land,
but you know where you are: Columbia!
Jerusalem is as far away as Mars.
Sumter, forty miles northeast, is even farther.
But your people are your people.
And if you wait, they will come to you
and bring gifts of candles to light up your eyes.
They will get off at the bus stop and walk you home.

The Girl Alone
Mark Brazaitis

The girls who lived next door to me didn't know her name. Olivia said she didn't have a name, although Elvira said her name was some kind of flower, Rosa or Orquidea or Girasol. They weren't sure where she lived, although Marta thought she came from the village of Chitul, and Olga guessed the village of Rìo Frìo. They called her "the girl who wants to be alone" because when they saw her she was always by herself, and when on a day they were feeling generous and asked her if she wanted to play, she'd shaken her head.

When I asked them to describe her, they gave only general words: black hair, brown skin, dark eyes. But when I asked them to compare her to themselves, they said she had Olivia's eyes—large, bright, and round—and Elvira's hair—thin, long, and black—and Marta's crooked, bright teeth and Olga's sweet laugh. Yes, they had heard the girl who wants to be alone laugh, and this puzzled the girls who lived next door to me because they wondered why she laughed.

The girls lived in a two-bedroom house with their cousin, Elda, their little brother, Josue, their little sister, Rut, and their mother, father, and grandmother. In the two rooms across the courtyard from their house lived their aunt Aura, their uncle Juan, and their other cousins, Edna, Claudia, Edvin, and Hugo. This type of crowding wasn't unusual in houses in Santa Cruz Verapaz, the town in Guatemala where I lived as a Peace Corps volunteer. Some families I knew slept three to a bed and nine to a room.

People in Santa Cruz asked me frequently if, living alone in my six-room house, I was lonely, and I always said no, although this wasn't always true. I was two thousand miles from home, and although I'd made many friends in Guatemala, I'd go weeks without hearing English spoken. In Guatemala, I read twice the number of books per week I did in college. At night I often played my guitar by candlelight, my bedroom serving as my private concert hall. Sometimes I stayed up past midnight listening to the Voice of America.

Olivia told me once she couldn't imagine spending even an afternoon alone in her house. The emptiness and silence, she said, would make her sad and afraid. As a North American, I had a different perspective on being alone. I came from a culture where "having your own space" is a crucial component of mental health. From the time I left my crib, I had my own room, and during my teens, it offered a haven from my parents' fights. I would shut the door, turn on music or open a book, and I was safe because I was alone.

I was curious about the girl Olivia and her sisters described, and one day we decided we would go look for her where they always saw her, in the calvario on top of the hill across from my house. The calvario was one of my favorite places. From its steps, a person could see the entire town. Santa Cruz was set in the middle of mountains, with trees shooting up between the two hundred or so houses, offering wings of shade. The calvario's twin aluminum doors were usually closed and locked, but sometimes they were open, and I would go inside and sit in front of the altar decorated with flowers in old milk cans.

We trudged up the hill three consecutive afternoons without seeing the girl who wants to be alone. But on the fourth day, from the bottom of the hill, Olivia spotted her in the belfry, her head resting against the curve of the bell. She was like they described her, except she seemed older than any of them. Like them, she was indígena, and she wore a worn blue corte and a faded, red güipil. The girls raced up the hill, yelling as if in a cavalry charge. Rosa or Orquidea or Girasol must have seen them because she quickly left the belfry.

We entered the calvario and found it dark and even gloomy, despite the broad windows on both the east and west walls. At the altar were dozens of flowers and an assortment of burned candles, and the place smelled of roses and wax. We looked around for several minutes before Olivia spotted her hiding between birds of paradise. Olga laughed, and Elvira and Marta shouted: "There she is! There's the girl who wants to be alone!"

Realizing how rude our intrusion was, I told the girls to be quiet. "Let's go outside," I said, and we left the calvario to sit on the steps. As the girls talked, I thought about the girl inside. I wondered whether she really wanted to be alone or if she was only shy. Pointing to the calvario, I said to Olivia, "Ask her if she wants to play."

A few moments later, Olivia returned. "She doesn't want to play."

"Why?"

"I don't know."

I wondered why a girl all alone in a temple with no toys wouldn't want to play. I couldn't resist: I told Olivia to ask the girl why she wanted to be alone.

Olivia came back with her reply: "She says she doesn't want to be alone and never is alone." Olivia shrugged. "She says she's with the flowers and the bell."

We agreed she was a strange girl, and after playing our games, we went home.

Sitting alone at dusk in my courtyard, I thought again about the girl who wants to be alone. I wondered about the things she was with, the flowers and the bell, and whether she imagined them talking to her like friends. Or were the flowers and the bell enough in themselves, I wondered, to make her feel she wasn't alone, the flowers fragrant and brilliant orange and red and blue and the bell firm and thick and smooth?

As night came, I began to see faces emerge from the mold on the walls, and I heard voices in the dripping faucet of my pila. But it was the rose bush in my garden I chose as my evening's companion. Tall, many-branched and blooming, it was as fixed as a friend and as sweet smelling as a lover.

"Snail"
Painting by Keith Abbott

Curandera
Lara Ramsey

The nuns entered the sick room in single file, the scent of dust
wafted in on their swishing skirts, black folds of illumination.
Even a savior dangling at their pious hips couldn't make right
the wrong that they had no egg. No blessed, ritual egg.

The nuns sat as two dark clouds, limbs melting into their bodies, melted
into *the* body, leaving only their soothing whispers and a promise
of healing draped about them like that ethereal halo about clouds that glows
less and less brilliant as sunset relinquishes sky to moonrise.

And all the while, that benevolent god at rest in his clean, sterile garden
stared shamelessly. A terrifying little mangod, his emaciated body—
broken and bloodied—smarted in young eyes as the waning sun,
through stained glass, refracted over cold silver or golden flesh.

Little mangod, you need an egg. Didn't your grandmother ever tell you?
An egg and the sea foam scent of aging flesh nearing as you stand or sit
or lie aching. The silent histories of your people mapped out
in the wrinkles that bless your grandmother's brow and cascade

down her face making an Indian tapestry of neck, throat and chest, then finish
their pilgrimage where steady finder tips greet glowing white circle.
And glowing white circle begins to undulate, moving through constellations

of secret syllables and sound clusters; moving through ancient codices and a song
of blood—drawing my center out, drawing it out of my center, drawing into its center
my center, leaving the circle about me white, leaving its center yellowed.

Once my grandmother had cracked the egg, she released its yellow center,
my center, into a flowered dish from the kitchen cupboard.
And so that the vanquished spirits would be less inclined to return,
she placed two sticks, in the image of a cross, above the bowl.

*(The curanderas of Mexico have many mystical means of curing all varieties of illnesses.
Sometimes something as simple as an egg is a powerful healing source.)*

from Poems for Harry
David S. Cho

*

Harry Kim awakens,
hears what might be the cooing
of birds in the early morning half light
yet dark, runs down the hallway

to see his father kneeled
before a chair as a pastor would
before an altar or pew.
He is praying, Harry discovers,

in a tongue that seems to come
from the heavens, or at least
the rafter of pigeons above.
And in silent reverence

which equals love for his father,
Harry imitates that strange roll
and garble of unintelligibles
in his mind and later through

his own lips. He practices them,
imagining their original meaning,
becoming a meditation of sorts,
a young child whose brows knit

together in a furrow, closing out
time, listening to the curtains unfold,
smelling the dust gathering
in rays through the open window slits.

*

Harry never saw his parents
hold hands, let alone

kiss, as sometimes the parents
of the neighborhood kids would

coming home before dinner.
But Harry would see his parents

sitting inches away
from another.

Mrs. Kim would roll sesame-oiled rice,
spinach, yellow pickled radish, and long

pieces of meat into a bamboo mat,
pressing the roll tight.

The slices, black
as a lacquer plate

hanging on their wall:
two silver men eating

from a pearl-potted rice,
the moon shining like a nickel.

Mr. Kim would watch
eyes half opened, as if to sleep,

how he loved to see the rolls sliced vertically,
the white, yellow and black slivers separating,

cut clean through the core, precise
as the rhythm of her "Amens"

uttered between the pauses
of her pastor and husband's prayer,

savored in the mouth
of a man who worked all night,

for the joy of coming home
to his wife,

who would take disparate items
and roll them together again

like a potter.

*

after Philip Levine

To know what work is,
watch Harry, a young boy

of age nine, burn his thumb
on the pot of water, check if it has boiled

enough to place a few beef franks in it,
boil them red, broth forming from the fat

and beef in its long sacks.
Watch Harry put the franks and its soup

in his father's thermos, pack a smaller thermos of coffee,
and a bag of rice, chanting to go with his father,

help him clean the spit, gum and mud of the kids he played
with at school, wash the windows clean, and make

what Harry's friends made black with their bowels and bladders,
porcelain white clear.

Watch Harry leave for school
as his father comes in from the third shift,

go to his study, pray for a while, letting his hands
straighten from the mop's hold, his hair dry out

from the sweat and ammonia, his mind cleaning out as he prayed
to his God for sweet rest, strength for the next night,

and many thanks for the money to take care of his family.
See his fingers callous over the years

and turn dark from the lack of oxygen.
See him stay up to study and prepare for the next

Sunday's message.
Watch Harry's eyes gleam when his father,

bagged eyes and all,
tells Harry that he drank down the food,

rice, meat, soup and all — it was good —
for it was made by his only son,

and that Harry must study hard,
prepare for the unexpected turn in life,

work hard as his father,
for, before the Lord,

that is what work is.

Eostre Sonnet
Rosemerry Wahtola Trommer

For thousands of years my Teutonic people built fires
atop the hillsides to honor Eostre, goddess
of dawn and spring, the shining deity
who wrestled life back from long winter, who coaxed
light back from burnt night. My people, they marked
the day that Eostre overcame the dead,
returning to their earth its vernal green
just as she had for every generation.

Today, I search beyond the plastic grass,
beyond marshmallow chicks and jelly beans.
I praise the reproductive rabbit, praise
the faultless egg. I light one candle at
our Easter table and remember how
the warmth of hillside fires thawed through the night.

Church
Ray Gonzalez

A man walks into a church and finds he is the only person in the dark sanctuary. He goes to the altar where several votive candles are quietly burning. He stops in front of a peeling statue of La Virgen de Guadalupe, bows down before the shrine, and makes the sign of the cross. Suddenly, a bat flies out of nowhere and streaks across the chamber. Startled, he follows the darting creature with his eyes as it disappears beyond the choir balcony. He turns back to the candles so he can pray, but is disrupted by a drop of water that lands on his sleeved arm. He looks up at the distant ceiling in time for a second drop to hit him on the chin because the roof is leaking from the silent rain falling outside. The man moves on his knees a couple of feet down the bench and begins his first Our Father. He is halfway through the prayer when an altar boy, mumbling incoherently, runs from the priest's chamber, his footsteps echoing through the church. The man is distracted again as the boy, dressed in his colorful frock, takes one of the small burning candles and returns to the back room. The man shakes his head at the trail of wax the boy drips on the floor. This time, he manages a complete Our Father and two Hail Marys before a dense cloud of incense fills the air around the statue. He begins to cough, and his eyes start burning. He rises to his feet and notices the poison sweetness of the incense is coming from the priest's chamber. He coughs and walks back there, but the incense makes him nauseous and he stops at the door. Inside, the altar boy is holding the ugly bat over the candle flame, its wings folded so it won't escape. Next to him, an old priest is crying and shaking his head, his clothes soaked from the rain, a pot of incense hanging from a rope in his outstretched hand. The man has had enough, turns and bolts down the long aisle between the pews. As he reaches the sanctuary doors, he spots the containers of holy water mounted on the walls. He can't resist and dips a finger into one of them, then raises the wet finger to trace a cross on his forehead. This sets off a loud clattering of wings behind him, but he does not turn to look. When he opens the door, it is early evening and the rain has stopped, everything under the sky is wet and shiny. Hundreds of bats pour out of an open window below the bell tower. They fill the sky as the man stands under the arch, not quite sure where he parked his car. Three more altar boys come up the concrete stairs toward him, and he gets out of the way as two priests embrace each other on the sidewalk near the street.

Ode to Nelly Sachs
Marilyn Kallet

If the prophets broke in
through the doors of night
and sought an ear like a homeland ...
would you hear?
        —Nelly Sachs, *O the Chimneys*

You rode your breath to the truth
while others kept silent
while others had no breath.

You were the voice
of doomed stars
of separations
and dust.
Your voice faced down
"evil nursemaids"
who replaced mother's milk
with terror.
You were a guardian
of our pulse still beating
of our memory.

You were an angel of truth
of "Israel's body
drifting up in smoke."
You would not close your eyes.
Darkness was too familiar.
You were sister
to the ashes.

"O the chimneys
 O the ingeniously devised
     habitations of dust..."
the loss of millions
on your lips.

You cradled the survivors
You broke through the doors
the years

Yes, we hear
your cry
your songs of healing
and remember them
like a homeland.

(Born in Berlin, Nelly Sachs (1891-1970) was the last Jewish poet to write in German until recent years. She fled to Stockholm in 1940. In 1966, she was co-winner with S.Y. Agnon of the Nobel Prize for Literature.)

Overnight at Quacamaya
Doug Evans Betanco

I write Palm Sunday morning, happy breezes on my face, off the fiery mountains of Honduras. My worn, painted table is from my new mother's *sala*, her altar to *Dios* and to *Catolico universal*. *Esta mañana,* she has offered it joyfully to me, "For your writing desk at the *finca*, Dugla!" and I have—with a look over my shoulder—accepted. It sits now for the day in the shade of her *orno*—oven—on the patio fronting the new house at the *finca*, the farm of *mi nuevo papa, don Moncho Betanco*, here in Nicaragua. I live at Quacamaya on the weekends this trip, arriving very early Saturday morning with the roosters crowing over all Teote, off in the hazy distance. Quacamaya has its own choir; one very nervy *gallo* struts at my feet, pecks my sandals.

Cesar and I appear dressed for work in worn jeans, to help my brother Denis build his new house and to help my father with another heavy project: we make our own adobe bricks—ivory-white—from the banks of the river Limon; we cut poles from the jungle of *Madera* and bamboo; we cement, with further mud, the dried adobes we have made, to the foundation of pebbles my father has laid, for two new rooms on the *finca's hacienda nueva*. The northern room of this addition will be a bedroom for my adopted parents, with a door connected to the long, great room of beds to its east. Next to this adobe boudoir, connected by a lockable door, a wide, well-lit room will rise, with two other doors, one to the gardens and one to the *sala*, my mother's living room. Both rooms have views to the western hills; both rooms can be self-contained. The second one is mine.

Stretching for thirty odd feet along the finca's west front, this new addition fosters many dreams: For *mi padres*, who have raised nine children and most of their offspring during twenty years of grueling *campesino* poverty, some well-deserved privacy, for Bible reading and whatever creaky but vital people do when they are alone; for me, a studio, with single bed, desk, a simple easel, and space for all my art supplies and current projects. I'll still do my writing at the studio in town, at my sister Marta's, but, soon, my drawings, paintings, sculptures will be here at Quacamaya, at the bend of the Rio Limon.

Of course, I'm flattered by *don Moncho's* gift: I've wanted to have a foot on the farm since I first saw it, the year I bonded with this resilient family here in Teote, with its charismatic leader. I immediately offered my hands to help, every step of the way. After all, no longer, thank the stars, will I need to sleep alone, crowded with the saints of Heaven, in my mother's *sala*.

These Saturday nights, I sleep over on a twin bed normally slept in by my sister Marivel and her two children, Gisele and Jose Arran. Their mosquito net protects me; their *pichinga*—night jar—and their bedroom, the sala of the hacienda, its sacred heart, with all the holy pictures in Nicaragua on its walls, become "mine." To them, it's an honor, and truly, if there were room, they would move behind the wall for good, preferring sleep chock-a-block, spoon-fashion, in the multiple beds full of brothers and sisters, *muchachos* galore, aunts, cousins and uncles, abuelas and don Moncho, all *Betancos*, dreaming together in the L-shaped room that wraps around the *sala*, to the north and the east. There are at least nine sleeping there full time, but when I come, it swells to thirteen, plus at least eight or nine others also staying over, Saturday night. On holy days, this can grow to thirty or forty. Plus, of course, the brooding chickens and their sleeping bands of chicks.

They all squash into that room instead of spilling over into the *sala* because they know I need my space, in the night, since I am, among other things, *a loco norteamericano*, albeit with a Nicaraguan heart. My need for solitude, a purely cultural phenomenon from an abundant life, they don't even want to understand. It's, to them, an aberration: The thought of sleeping alone in the Nicaraguan night even petrifies them; it would never allow them to sleep—it's just not done. Their culture, which I find so easy to share in most respects, pretty much sets me down here. I need my space. And so, they joyfully give it to me, while at the *finca* now. I take it as a signal honor, with only a wee twinge of selfish guilt thrown in. I still feel a usurper, sometimes, in the night.

It doesn't help that I go to bed much earlier than the rest of the family when I'm here because my daily labor is more taxing than my all-day-half-the-night stints at the writing desk in Teote. Writing, remember, is my bliss: I can't get enough of it. It writes my life very well. Indeed, it energizes me, keeps me awake with future words demanding to be instantly put down. Digging mud all day, on the other hand, has me sore, pooped, depleted, and I am headed to the sack by seven, an hour after sundown, after a droll farewell from half my assembled familia Betanco, sitting on benches and red plastic *sillas*, joking softly underneath the most enchanted Nicaraguan moon. I'm beat. They know it; we laugh. I head for the *sala*.

At the *finca*, my bed rests against the southern wall, the only other furniture in the room her sacred altar, her house of humble prayer. I wear the clothes I'm in, like any good Nicaraguan, exchanging them for clean when I bathe in the *rio* in the mornings, leaving dirty ones for the *lavadora* to wash in the river and hang out to dry in the hot, midday sun. Off come the sandals and socks, and into *mi cama* I go.

My mother, as always, has lit a candle at her shrine, though a bit early, in preparation for my coming. I thank all that is, lying under my sheet, turn towards the wall. It's amazing how bright one candle can be in an otherwise very dark room. I close my eyes and Sania, thirteen, starts reading her homework by its light at the table.

She's snuck in on little cat's feet, sat down with her notebook, and is correcting an essay in English for me, due on Monday. She is a very good student of the language. Unfortunately, when she reads it, she mouths it, forming every blessed word as I have taught her, whispering loudly in the candlelight. She's having a problem with tenses and irregular verbs, it's clear. She hisses, "Ran' or 'Runned'?" a few times, waits, then, a bit more loudly, repeats the question softly, again. "Ran," I say, wearily, turning once again to the wall and letting out a deep, low sigh. She gets the picture and takes her homework to the kitchen, where, of course, every night but tonight, apparently, she sits and works for two or three hours, learns catechism for her first communion, studies for tests at the high school—on a scholarship from me—and practices her English on every passerby.

Sania on her own, I nestle up against the wall and count my blessings, grumpily. Then, I forgive the world—including myself—for not being perfect, and, sighing loudly, try to shuffle off to Never-Never Land.

Twenty minutes later, the hordes of Babylon descend upon the sala, all on little cat's feet, whispering, one after another, *"Buenas noches, Douglas."* I know that it will enhance their honor to feign sleep, now, the happy result of all their active quiet for an hour, so I snore lightly through this rather than replying. With only a few, cooing jokes about my "sweet-baby snoozes" from the little girls, they head for the back bedroom, on the other side of the *sala*'s opposite wall, giggling and sh-sh-ing all the way.

Hundreds of *muchachos* later, several brothers and sisters, whispering "Good night, Douglas," and *mi padre*—oohing about my peacefulness—tiptoe past. Don Moncho wishes "Good dreams, *mi hijo*"—my son—and closes the bedroom door.

"That's got to be everyone," I exult, to myself. Once again, I am alone in the *sala*. I am aglow with *gracias* to the U. and to half my family in Teote. What a pleasant, dry, delightful group of *campesinos* they are!

A bull snorts—mightily—in the pasture.

Pigeons coo.

A breeze riffles the palms in the orchard.

Of course, thousands of Betancos are currently getting ready for bed, together, thanking each other, saying prayers most softly over each other's murmurs in the adjacent room. We may have a wall between us, but that's all there is, since there is no ceiling, and the open-raftered house—filled with little bat wings in the dark—hears it all. There are, seriously, at least fifty Nicaraguans—*mas o menos*—from Teote, from Somoto, from even Managua, and from far away Bluefields on the Caribbean coast, here this weekend, at the beginning of Holy Week, especially to meet Douglas, *el norteamericano angelico de Dios*, talking in *susurros*—whispers—right next to my tired head. A few, low grunts from the bellies of five *grosseras*, my sainted sisters, menace sharply, hiss with passion: "*Silencio, chunchas, para* Douglas!" By this time, I am having absolutely the best of times, giggling under my hands, into my pillow, badly—but successfully—holding it in: my stomach aches with silent laughter. I wouldn't have one of those *grosseras susurrandas* hauling off on me for riling *los niños, por nada*!

In the pasture, the bull, Negrito, groans so loudly, and for so long, everyone shuts up to listen. Then, *mi padre* tells a whispered cow *caca* joke about this bull which produces gales of muffled belly laughs, all helpless, but held under fifty pillows, on fifty wet shoulders. It's as if a silent earthquake is shaking the house. I have stuffed my sheet into my mouth, since the *pobrecito* who had backed into this bull's huge pile of steaming *caca* in his bare feet that afternoon was the Angel from *Los Estados*, me. This happens every day.

Finally, we all quiet down again.

Then, eight-year-old Mildria, a little whiney for a Nica child, cries loudly that she needs to go potty—rather plaintively, I might add—and three *grosseras* from the fields hiss, "Hold it!" as one. I am in stitches, but also a tad bit desperate for her and for my breath. Luckily, I recognize the moment for a *urina* joke and hiss right back, with a very loud groan, "Give her my *pichinga*," out of the blue, and the whole *adobe casa* rolls and rocks in shock waves of happy pandemonium, for 20 minutes—count them!—swear to God.

I'm a great hit in Nicaragua, and I thank everything there is, ten times a day, for this great, good fortune. It's the Palladium in London: I'm the star.

Eventually, we all reuse our *pichingas*, clear our throats, settle in, *una mas vez*. No more ripples of laughter, leading to gusts. It's almost quiet in the house. Even Negrito has given up, out in the fields. I can hear the river singing in the dark.

Then, my niece Gisele, in whose borrowed bed I lie when at the finca, whispers, *"Buenas noches, mi abuelo,"* to don Moncho. He whispers, *"Buenas noches, mi Gisele,"* with such sweetness, from his bed. Gisele then carefully says "Good night" to everyone who's there, one by one, with softly spoken, appropriate responses, and a couple "Don't Forgets" from her mother. This takes about ten minutes, perhaps the most endearing ten minutes of my life, to date. I am living "The Waltons," I realize, and everything is fine at Walton's Mountain for one more day. I keep expecting someone to say, "Good night, John-Boy." She ends, however, with me, most honored heavenly being with his own space in the other room, with a *"Buenos noches, Tio* Douglas," with a long-drawn yawn in between, and I reply, *"Buenas noches, mi familia,* sweet dreams." As a choir, they all whisper, *"Y usted,"* and I am swimming in the warmth of the oceans of the world, one with all its treasures, a tear in my eye.

Immediately, the room next door is silent. This round of Gisele's is her special privilege in the night at Quacamaya this year, and believe me, she does it with honor, a little pride. It is the signal that it's time for sleep, and everybody does.

"But one," I sigh in silence, turned to the wall. The candle still burns. *"Silencio,* darkness," I pray.

But, no.

Creeping on little cat's feet, *mi madre* and Sania, who, I guess, have been quietly cleaning up in the kitchen all this time, appear at my feet in the *sala.* They creak the door shut, and silently build a barricade behind it, locking up the room. Then, they glide to the altar on their knees, Bibles in hand, and begin their nightly prayers: to *Dios,* to *El Señor,* to Maria, to *Espiritu Santo;* to all the saints and martyrs, the angels, too; to all the churches of the world—"Special Thanks;" to Rome, for a Polish benediction; to all *los pobrecitos* and *los ricos* of the world—"Special Peace;" to the people of *Los Estados*—"Special *Gracias,"* magnified for the people of my hometown in Colorado; and, for Douglas, the blessing of *Dios,* for the great *"gracia de Dios para todos"*—for all. They ask for aid and benediction, in return, and kiss the feet of the Madonna standing there, a gift from me.

It is a gracious moment, though I feel like a CIA spy, snooping in on their private prayers. Of course, they know I'm there and would have it no other way, *gracias a Dios.* More truthfully, it is forty holy minutes, one for every day, they say, that Jesus spent in the wilderness, struggling for the sake of us all.

It is also the beginning of *Semana Santa,* I realize anew; tomorrow is *Domingo de Ramos,* Palm Sunday, the day he entered Jerusalem so many years ago and took the holy city by storm for five strange days, having made his decision to die. It is the holiest of many holy weeks in Nicaragua: Easter in Teote, a long-awaited, new experience for me, has begun.

While I'm reflecting, *mi madre*—bless her heart—and Sania wrap it up with a whole Hail Maria, really fast, kiss her feet once more, give me the cross, and whisp away, close the door, off to their own silent, very happy beds. They creak into *camas*, loaded with at least fifty Betancos. Not a peep.

The silence of *Dios* wraps the house. It is finally as quiet as a tomb, yet crammed with people, living on faith in eternal life. *"Buenas noches,* Douglas," they say.

Dona Eva, in the one great extravagance of her very rich/very poor life, leaves the cheap candle burning at the feet of the Virgin, till it's out. It's in a silver candlestick I brought for her a couple of years ago. She buys these candles by the dozen for pesos, marked "For special, long praying." They usually gutter in thirty minutes, but this last one, by some miracle, burns for at least an hour, maybe more. Perhaps she lights another, but I have watched more than once to make sure and have not seen it. Must be angels.

Through all the winged prayers on her knees—then, for twenty minutes more—it flickers on the altar, six feet from my head. I turn in my bed to face it, use it to write in my prayer journal. My family thinks I'm asleep, but I'm as awake as any *suplicante* can be. I wait its dying moment, almost regretfully, hopefully in love with Nicaragua and the world, and all the *chunchas* in it. The night has become a holy moment. Time stills. I sit in *mi cama*, borrowed for just this occasion, aching for sleep, aching to stay awake; wanting the dark but loving the light this candle shines on my life; listening to snoring next door and to other angel noises in the rustling of bats and *palomas* in the eaves, in the lowing of cattle, in the quiet noise of the Nicaraguan night.

Tomorrow, I reflect, all my family in Teote—all ninety-three—will gather at the *finca de Quacamaya* for lunch, then troop to the ancient little church in the distant city for their palms, from the traveling Padre Fredis. He's about as Methodist as any priest from Jalapa can be, preaching Jesus the *pobrecito, amigo,* and brother as well as Lord, a "personal savior who speaks to us all in our hearts"; It's as Protestant, as Catholic, as "New Age" as can be, this message of hope and inner guidance. The cathedrals in Managua and Rome have banned "liberation theology" as heresy, but apparently, in "Sandinistaville," that word hasn't come. Of course, I'll go, too. *En Teote, yo soy Catolico.*

At Quacamaya, there will be much to clean, much to cook, much to do on Palm Sunday morning, even though it is an official day of rest for all Teote. It will start with the roosters, at five *en la mañana*. Before the sun rises red from all the smoke of pines ablaze in the hills during this dry season, there will be baking of *rosquillas*, rich egg, and corn cookies; fifty dirty T-shirts to wash in the river and dry for church, and many dirty, slippery little bodies. Then, the feast of *tamales* and *sopa de mentira*, a soup " that lies" because it has corn and potato *tortas*, simulating meat, it being *Semana Santa*.

Afterward—"*Pues, si!*"—we will all take an hour's siesta—only on Sundays—in the sweltering heat of the day, before the sacred mass starts at three.

The *candela de milagros* finally gutters, dies. I put my pen down; my prayer journal closes at the end of another day. It is at least 11 P.M. In it I have "taken dictation," as I call these perfect dialogue/poem/prayers. Here, they always come *en Espanol*:

Al Señor, Noche Antes de Ramos, Quacamaya

"Gracias, Douglas, con la gracia de Dios."
"Ay, de nada, Señor, a La Orden, para servirté, Señor."
"Para servirte, también, gracias de Dios."
"Y usted, Señor, a usted! Mis gracias, al Señor."
"A Dios, Douglas: de Dios, por Dios, con Dios, para Dios, Douglas."
"A Dios, Señor, y, por favor, Señor, a mi cama, Señor?
"Adiós, gracias de Dios."
"Buenas noches, Douglas, a Dios, adiós."
"Gracias, Señor, con la gracia de Dios."

Finally, I join my family—and all the other angels—in peace over the tumult of night at the *finca Quacamaya*; within the hushed heart of *Dios*, even in Dona Eva's *sala*, I sleep.

"Monkey"
Painting by Keith Abbott

Tattoos

Gordon Johnston

God, to be a page, letters in my skin, not under it, sandy ink mingled and
clotted with my blood into permanence, word made flesh in me, on me,
so that I'm a tombstone, a paint rock, a heart-carved tree slowly warping
my lover's name with my own growth. In Haggadah, each letter of the alphabet
begged God to let the world be wrought through her. Beta won.
Be: saying it made all so. Words must be left as evidence, to ease
the loneliness in places or to sharpen it, to needle in our passage through.
Our bodies, subways, bridges, boulders, great granite hills written,
branded, worked with proof souls live there—souls needing not dead wood
to write on but the first and last thing to write on: this body. The print
just deep enough never to be shed, to blur ink and blood into *Mother*,
Love, Jesus wept, stars, roses and chinese dragons. Notes for the final.

Imago Dei
Jim Elledge

God who sings one pure note, only one, over
and over, each note to punctuate the pause
between each thud of my heart's beat God
who listens to the note's echo—and *its* echo:
a duet God who blinks once and sets the
world into a metronome's rhythm, day to
night, night to day, and back again God who
rains a soft spiccato across a meadow dawn to
noon then lifts it skyward—a slick glissando
until dusk God who puffs the sky full with
its blue, the sky that's utterly empty God
who strolls the aisles between lawn and the fog
rolling in upon it God who strolls along the
border between dawn and day then day and
dusk God who lounges in the second between the year's last moment and the next
year's first God who stands between a lit candle's wick and its flame God who murmurs
His autobiography in the space between the *I*
of "In the beginning" and the *n,* between the
birth groans of the beasts and brutes and the
canticles of the angels God who moves like
weather across land and water, mountain
and plain God who pirouettes atop a junk
heap's apex—without disturbing a tin can, an
old Buick chassis, a duct-taped La-Z-Boy,
wadded up paper bags and crushed milk car-
tons, faux Persian rugs, aluminum Christmas trees, or powder blue commodes God
who tap dances—top hat and cane—atom to
atom up each swell then down each trough
of the Pacific, star to star across the universe
God who loves the bonsai and Mt. Everest
God who loves Victor the Wild Child of
Aveyon God who loves the horizon line
when, as He holds His thumb between the

sky and Him, it merges into the deepest
wrinkle on His thumb God who loves the
mirror because, before Him, it's worthless
God who loves delirium as if it were a blue
flower full of fragrance and passion as if it
were a pawn shop's window covered by an
accordion grate God who loves the seven
oceans that gnaw at the beaches of each of the
seven continents, then toss what they've
taken back God who loved Galileo at the tele-
scope, Newton beneath the tree, Curie at the
microscope, and Darwin in the Galápagoes,
their formulae and theories song, *song!* sung
by a tiny voice

Cardinal Points

Mary Sullivan, r.c.

Slate blue
indigo ink blue
cohabit
pre-dawn sky.
Crescent moon
cradles
Venus tear drop.
I walk
conscious
last night's constellations
in the black firmament
gone.
Earth's move changes familiar bearings.
Streaks and clots of color
tenant
my spirit.
A plaintive keen
rants, rails, rends.
O Orient
must I sever
cherished tethered moorings
if you are to rise
give compass to my life?

Illumination
Kathy Kennedy Tapp

In the humid half dark of
      first night
a brief pinpoint of light
   for space of one breath,
     then
         gone.

I search the sky,
   stumble through dark grasses,
glimpse another quick
        flash.

Where are you?

The shadowy field
     transforms
    to a sparkling realm—
bright energy points
     explode everywhere,
    a thousand starry
          blinks.

   Presence.
Teasing, comforting, coaxing.

  Firefly God,
  You are everywhere,
        playing   tag.

   Blink on inside me.

Benedictus
Susan Thomas

at the Benedictine Monastery

My sorrow is alive here
but it has a sweeter taste.
I don't believe what the sisters believe,
but I believe in their belief, their wish
to love whatever there is, their faith
in what isn't there. What can I stake
my faith on? Complicated hearts
tangle in the undergrowth and
they must find their way in the dark,
through the scrape and tussle of love.
The sisters sing Benedictus,
everything melts into sound:
  kyrie elieson sanctus elieson

Janet's Prayer
Davi Walders

Noon is cold and full of sun. Trying to pray for you, Janet, I watch bulldozers and backhoes knock down the house across the street, the one we used to stare at as we sat and rocked, rocked and talked, talked and worked together. I am thankful, dear friend, that you didn't laugh when I said I would pray for you—I, a Jew, you a Catholic, both of us fallen away more times than bricks tumbling across the street.

I am trying to find some way to stay with you a thousand miles away in that sterile room where they are drilling through your cranium in search of a tumor which branches exquisitely, you say, just like the oak tree across the street. You say you saved the x-ray film, will frame the tumor's mysterious beauty, hang it in your office. Just to remember, you say, if you survive.

To answer your question, yes, I did notice a stumble or two, a slur, a drift, but we're in our fifties and who am I, forever forgetting things, banging into furniture and people, to find it odd. We're all odd and getting odder. In the restaurant, we still laughed. Just another bit of slowing down, I thought, not a tumor speeding up.

I am sitting where we have so often sat, watching. Now, Janet, everything is down, tree stumps and rubble carted off. Sure the house needed work, and perhaps the trees were a bit weary, but something could have been saved. Now there is only one tree left, roped off with a fence tied with pink ribbons, fought for and saved by neighbors. Yellow cranes and dusty dump trucks fill the space. All else is gone to make room.

Is this prayer, Janet, to speak of gravel and regrading instead of pleading with G-d for what I want? I want you well, to sit together again, laughing, cursing at the work we have to do, then glancing up to watch that huge oak play host to ivy and a black squirrel scurrying down toward hidden nuts. Can I pray by telling you of one last tree amidst dirt and dumpsters?

I will keep my eye on those pink ribbons fluttering around the oak, the squirrel scampering there and let my heart do its work, willing you well, will you here. When you come in spring, perhaps the buzz saws will be gone. Perhaps there will be a garden with low flowering cherries as the new couple has promised. Perhaps young trees will be in full pink bloom. Perhaps.

These are only words, Janet, like I promised. Words about trucks, a tree, things old and new. Words about aging, anger, loss. And hope—hope that right things remain and wrong things are removed. This is a prayer for you, Janet. I hope.

Ghazal of White
Rachel Dacus

Flare of apple scent, ancient caress. A wind arose within
and silently calls me home to the White Rose within.

Silence is music's white heart. Through its blaze pass all sounds,
returning to the beloved Gaze that grows within.

Sunlight animates cell and eye, but cannot match
the gold that leaped from His touch and now glows within.

I'm after the whiteness that winnows essence from pith,
a mysterious wind of love that blows within.

Give up your white lies. We are fish in an ocean of God.
Why whisper, when your every thought he knows within?

Rose of Silence, You are the fulcrum of absence
and fullness, the perfect balance one rarely knows within.

White blossom, your offering is a divine hint
of the flowering that, petal by petal, unfolds within.

Oh, Rachel, bleach the veils, unthread your wishes and put your hand
in God's. As desire dies, its gold marrow is disclosed within.

Chantico
Ray Gonzalez

Chantico—she who dwells in the house.
Aztec goddess of hearth and volcanic fire.

For now we see through the dark mouth,
a difficult question stealing hunger
from the splintered tongue,
copper plates showing Chantico
disrobing her mind against a tree,
forcing her lover to repeat her thoughts
as he returns to the adobe.

For now we believe everything is taken,
a bloodstain on the mammal that ate the dirt,
sensing it was the remains of a marriage—
trails of flowers translated as paths to the volcano
where the fire is an easy playground,
the man who believes in the future sewing
his burned body to the museum wall.

For now we stare into her spine
and are called by our given names,
the sound of the leaning light hiding
the others who came before us, preceding
a weather of October's ashes, Chantico spent
on the arms of one man she didn't want
to bring back, his shivering thighs
touching her magma as a sign of love.

The Argument
Judith Lavezzi

The day began simply, but deteriorated.

The experience of his anger, the rational disappointment of their life together when he finally expressed it to her, felt as though it were taking place in another, strangely disconnected body. She vaguely felt herself pulled toward the scene where she stepped in front of the car, hearing the *pop!* her own blunted thud of body against steel, the bloodless, guiltless exit. She watched the accident, which was remarkably sound free, and thought how easy and clean it was.

"And," he said, "I have wanted to talk about the lack of communication when we are together, the sadness of the loss of our special time together, the meaningful glance across the room wherein we each could read the other's mind. The difficulty of keeping an 'us' together the way we once did, the pure selfishness of wanting all of your time and love, and yes, sex too."

Her vision took flight, the separation from the body going into the back yard where she was floating, fully clothed; swirling blue and gold chiffon about her, on the surface of the rippled rectangle of pool. She was found, no doubt, by a neighbor, for who else would have looked upon the dramatic sight of the woman, laying like a fall leaf, face down since dusk till this dawn. No awful scenes good bye, not one tear, just an exit out of the failure to be different than she was.

How could this be, the perfect sense of happiness, the commitment to the future, the commitment to a bonded eternity, what was it, anyway? To remain love-fevered, to have deep enjoined happiness; did it require disavowing the others that one loved, denying the connections to those unconnected others? And if true, how could one be but dead inside, and useless.

"I would like to have lunch together," he said "without there being everyone else talking to you, and you thinking that you have to give them of your time, though I know, when I am mature about it, that is pretty small, and unrealistic."

She laid on the surface of the pool, thinking peaceful cool water blurs, angelfishes swimming in sweet duets of wide eyed mutual protection.

She ached with the effort to swim.

Blood Skull Saddle
Martin Scott

Black Kali's riding, flame dripping peeled flesh,
      The inside of an arm, clean hair like dirty
Grave water, demons stretched across frayed light.
        The skulls dangle from froggy mouths earthy

And deciduous, you're certain you're unworthy
      Of skin that will not fall, of Autumn's fresh
Remembrances, the pikes and the blue highway
        Turning around the ruined statuesque

And royal body of The Moment, knife edge
        And madness, dead leaf and horse as close as skin.
The Thing Insane will make us Flesh, the Wedge

Of Ghost, enormous architecture of Sin,
      The VCR's and satellites besiege
The palms, the furthest reach of Crazy Tongue...

Mandalas, flame and leaf, the sharpened Word...

"Buddha"
Artwork by Joan Cantwell

The Year I Became Buddhist
Joan Cantwell

Prologue

I'm not sure when the wheel of dharma began to turn for me. I think it was when, as a young nurse, I went on R&R to Bangkok, to get away from my work in a Cambodian refugee camp. I bought a silver necklace of Buddha there and wore it until I lost it years later. I had my mother worried. "Are you becoming a Buddhist?" she suddenly asked me while we walked down the cereal section of the Jewel, two months after I'd returned from Thailand. I laughed and wanted to say "That should be the least of your worries." Why not ask me about the limbs blown off from land mines, or the time Thai soldiers stopped our cars "just to check," or the sounds of shelling that still echoed in my mind so that whenever I heard a fire cracker, or a car back up, I broke out in a cold sweat. And what about my transition back to the United States? "Any trouble with parasites?" she could have asked. "Maybe just a hint of depression?"

Those questions I could answer, wanted to answer, was begging to answer. The exotic necklace at my neck, after all, was just a souvenir. No, I wasn't ready for Buddhism, not ready for real compassion. And so I said nothing. And I thought the world was fucked as I stood in the grocery aisle and counted twenty-five different brands of perfectly aligned cereal boxes.

Blue Heart

It is now December twenty years later. While my mother and I wander through an outdoor garden store, I see a large cement statue of Buddha and buy it immediately. Amazingly, my mother once again asks, "Are you becoming a Buddhist?" This time I think yes but say nothing.

Although I had my own meditation practice for several years, I had recently started meditating with a Buddhist community. I found meditating with a group to be a powerful and interesting experience. But still, I didn't want to become a Buddhist, I just wanted to meditate with them.

Although I was not interested in the Buddha, it seems he was interested in me. And to my surprise began to slowly creep into my life. First he started playing with my mind. One night, he spoke to me as I was meditating at home, alone. I was holding a small plastic icon of the blue Buddha, the Buddha of healing. I sat in the dark with one candle lit. After sitting an hour, I heard the Buddha speak "I am fire, pure fire. I burn forever. I am ocean, deep spirit, cobalt blue. I am sky unfixed, ever changing. I am earth, deep clay, solid, fully acknowledged."

OK, he had my attention.

Then a few days later, he started in on my soul. I had gone to the Art Institute of Chicago. Heading down the hall of Indochinese art, the first thing I saw was a large Tibetan Thanka hanging of the blue Buddha. I cautiously approached the wall hanging and stared at the image. He was deep blue, the earth was on his right side, the moon was on his left. He held one hand in the gesture of praise, and the other held a medicinal plant indicating his commitment to heal the world. With an overwhelming sense of awe, I felt him beckoning me to enter the image.

I imagined the two of us alone in an ancient zendo, frozen in time. I smelled rain-scented incense, stood before him and pleaded with him "Align my soul."

I saw him smile and bow in silence. As I turned to leave, I was overcome with a great stillness, a place beyond chaos, before the days of anguish.

Lent: Three Dreams

Then there were the dreams I had in April every Thursday night during lent—following "The Life of Buddha" classes I had started taking at the local Zen temple.

In the first dream, I had been thinking of leaving the Catholic church to become a Buddhist and the pope came to visit me. He was young and strong and seven feet tall. I was completely impressed that he was at my house but nervous he might discover that I was thinking of becoming a Buddhist. I walked over to him and stared up at his chest. He bent over, placed his hand on my head and recited a Hail Mary. I awoke, laughed, then I cried. I got up and groggily walked to my studio to look at eight of my drawings: four Buddhas and four virgin Marys that I had drawn as part of my new art project.

The next Thursday, I dreamt that three apostles came to my house for dinner. We sat at my dining room table, drank wine, ate pasta with marina sauce, and they talked about how important the Catholic faith was. As usual, they did all the talking.

After the last "Life of Buddha" class, I dreamt that the far religious right wanted to end the world. I heard them plotting on a CTA bus. Then they started chasing me through the streets, through the corridors of a hotel and into a closet where I hid, trembling in fear. Dead flies lined the threshold of the door .When I awoke, I automatically went to my studio and created a birthday card for a friend using the face of the blue Buddha.

I thought I could duplicate it, make it into wrapping paper. Maybe send the pope a gift wrapped in it.

Good Friday

It was the fourth week of lent and three classes into "The Life of Buddha." My boss, the lifeline to a job change in which I suddenly had responsibility for in a subject I knew nothing about, had just quit. A few of us took him out on Good Friday for a beer, actually three, at Callaghans and sat drinking in a noisy, smoke-filled room. My boss was bitter and angry.

"Seventeen years down the drain" he said as he finished his 6th beer, and left the bar. Then my colleague Jim started in, talking about his fears, and disappointments. He said "we" (meaning I) needed to start putting in longer hours because "we" were "after all, managers." He did not flinch when I told him I already work ten-hour days. Smoke penetrated my eyes. I tried to remain calm but suddenly my monkey mind was now in control. Fueled with fear, it went wild. The volume in the bar rose as the afterwork crowd streamed in. The news blasted in the background. I felt raw and nauseated and watched the clock tick closer to 6:30 P.M. I told him I had to leave for Good Friday services. I left the bar, hailed a cab, and welcomed the fresh air. "St. Patrick's Church," I told the cab driver. "Going to church?" he asked. "Yep" I answered.

"You Catholic?" I did not answer but looked pensively out the window.

Reeking of tobacco and beer, I greeted my friend Marilyn on the door steps of the church. "You drunk?" she asked. " No," I lied. We listened to a monotone reading of the passion. Good Friday had always been special to me in the past; I always felt a sense of reverence and calm no matter what was happening in my life. And, after all, it was Jesus's top performance. I searched for inspiration in the priest's remarks, but all I could hear was his shouting. Did he shout because he thought we could not hear him? And why did he snap his fingers at us and move his hands artificially in wild exaggerated gestures? His voice throbbed inside my head. My voice throbbed inside my head. I wanted to scream back at him, wanted to tell him to sit down, stop shouting, and instead listen to the silence. And then I prayed that we all just sat in silence. That my monkey mind had found peace. That the entire church took one deep breath together, and we did not rush to fill in the spaces of understanding.

Then my exhausted mind drifted to my cement Buddha sitting at home, alone on my deck. I saw him sitting stoically in silence in the rain and cold. And that night, when I went home, I would sneak like a child to my kitchen window, step up on the tips of my toes, and lean out the window so that I could see him sitting, smiling peacefully, gently lit by my porch light. I saw him silently waiting for me.

The next week I fell in love with all suffering beings, wanted to have sex with anyone in pain.

My Buddhist Name

A month later in May, during the Precepts Taking Ceremony, I received my Buddhist name, Ch' A Dong, translated as "This thing always the same, everything returns to one." As the priest Sunim said when he gently placed the meditation beads around my neck, "You will have to discover what this name means." I touched the wooden beads, brought them to my face, and breathed in the scent of cedar. The smell lingered on my fingers then dissolved with the smell of burning incense from the altar. Ten minutes of Pali chanting rang through the temple. That might have been the moment, the one sacred moment I would remember forever, the moment when I felt connected with the entire universe. Nirvana, the moment every great Boddsavata waited for. But instead, all I could think was "Thank God my mother's not here."

And so I took the precepts. I resolved not to harm but to cherish all life: not to take what is not given but to respect the things of others; not to engage in sexual promiscuity but to practice purity of mind and self-restraint; not to lie but to speak the truth; not to partake in the productions and transactions of firearms and chemical poisons, nor of drugs and liquors that confused and weaken the mind; not to waste but to conserve energy and natural resources; not to harbor enmity against the wrongs of others but to promote peace and justice through non-violent means; not to cling to things that belong to me but to practice generosity and the joy of sharing.

After the ceremony, the twenty other new Buddhists and I nervously exchanged names and gave interpretations of what we thought they meant. I was grateful I did not get "Awkward fellow stumbling towards enlightenment" or "Urgency." We drank tea from miniature-sized cups and ate donated girl scout cookies. We congratulated one another, and three hours from the time the ceremony began, completely exhausted, we left the temple. I gazed up at the moonlight illuminating the branches of a nearby oak tree and wondered what it would feel like to walk into work the next day with my new commitment to see things clearly, seek the truth, confront fear, and remain unattached to the unraveling security of my seemingly organized, well paid, overworked life.

Green Bones and Baseball

I hate going to baseball games, even at Wrigley Field, the greatest outdoor ball park in North America. I just find the game boring. Am I un-American? And then there are the fans, thousands of people packed into the stands, spilling beer on one another. But that warm day I had agreed to go because it was a once-a-year team-building function for work. I sat next to a suburban woman who complained nonstop about her car being towed the night before. At the seventh inning stretch, I got up to use the washroom and never returned.

It was a beautiful spring day, and I decided to walk the few miles home. That's when I passed the Vietnamese temple. A bright yellow run down building with a red roof and door. I had always found this intriguing. I tried to open the door, but it was locked. I was about to walk away when I saw a very small hand-written sign near a button that read "ring bell." I did and was greeted by a tall, older Vietnamese man who, once I explained that I was a Buddhist and even had a name, let me in. Inside the temple were three large golden statues, a Buddha in the middle with a companion on either side. He explained that at this temple they do prostrations rather than meditations. He invited me to join the temple members at 6:45 a.m. each Sunday morning to do 108 prostrations, each one representing the name of Buddha.

He then led me to the back of the temple where a young monk in brown robes greeted me. His face lit up as I explained I was recently given a Buddhist name. He sat me down and explained the different sects of Buddhism and the different realms of the underworld each composed of animals, hungry ghosts, and hell. He drew the circle of birth, death, and rebirth on a brown piece of paper and then drew a line through the circle separating the top from the bottom. The goal he said was to escape the under world, to stay in the upper realms of human, asuras, and gods.

I thanked him for sharing all the information. He then asked me if I would like to see a relic of Buddha that his teacher had recently given him. "It is very rare, and not many people have seen it," he whispered. He hurried to a room behind the temple like an excited child about to share a rare baseball card collection. When he returned, he held a small red and gold pillbox and very gently lifted off the lid. In the middle of the box was a small ivy-colored gem, a particle of the Buddha. He explained to me that if a person reached "Pureland," if they are truly an enlightened human, then when they are cremated their remains will not burn but instead turn to gems. To prove this he went to his room a second time and brought back a small jar filled with four small green stones. He said that these were the remains of a enlightened member of that temple who had repeated the Buddha's name several hundred times before he died.

He took out the tiny stones one by one and gently placed them on the palm of my hand. We both smiled and stood in silent intimacy. I stared at the stones astonished and thought of the suburban woman from the baseball game probably wondering where I was. I wanted to shout, "Here I am! I'm holding the remains of an enlightened being," and have those words fly out the red temple door, down Damen Avenue, into Wrigley Field and echo over the entire ball park.

The young monk interrupted my fantasy by saying "Don't stay attached to anything. Only then will your mind be ignited and your heart free."

I gently placed the fragments back in their container, bowed, and said, "I must go." And as I was putting on my shoes, a small, wrinkled nun in a gray robe scurried out from the kitchen and handed me a brown paper bag with eight oranges in it. "These are for you," the young monk said with a smile. My mind flashed back twenty years ago to Thailand where I never left camp without a gift from one of the Cambodian refugees.

For one moment I was completely safe, and I was happy.

As I left, I bowed to the monk, hugged the bag of oranges to my chest, pulled the door closed, and walked away wondering what color my bones will be when I die.

And the Wheel of Dharma Turned.

Amen

"Cambodian Nuns with Offerings"
Photo by Willa Schneberg

An Agnostic Reads the Book of Psalms
Seth A. Steinzor

1

The psalmist, given by his life to know
to whom he owes it and the way, oh God,
to address his support and chief repose
in clear and simple agony of longing

sings past my hearing. All his higher notes
are lost on me. At what he so devotes
his voice, I cannot say, although his words
may cross my lips more easily, perhaps, than

he from whom they were wrenched could emit them.
I pause only at what I do not know:
the meaning, not the words. They seem so much
the same one poem to the next, each dreary

hysteric plea to crush whoever seeks
the psalmist ill, each childlike, prattling praise
to Whom spring grass, the sky, and vengeance all
are due; these words won't sink beneath the surface,

they bob and float before my eyes as light
and dead as balsa logs. I cannot bridge,
the way he does, this living river with
such forms of plea and praise. Swimming,

unsure of touching *terra firma*, sure
alone of some day touching bottom, where,
profundis, he has also been, I hope
the water each stroke fills my palms with also,

as his last breaths fled upward, filled his lungs,
and that the light he then saw is the one
that, broken on the flowing cusp of each
elusive wave, my eyes can't put together.

2

The god who could permit the Holocaust
is that same one who ordered Canaan cleared
of all its people. Broken light, that crossed
between the slats in cattle cars, as hard to

collect into coherent vision as
those blood-splashed desert rocks that not yet flowed
with milk and honey. Boggle at despair?
The note that strained the psalmist's throat yet higher

was just this one. It drove his faith's escape.
But if my bubble bursts before it finds
the sky, is it my fault? I might have been
recast as soap that disappears in water,

that scrubbed a moral dullard shining pink,
all melted, leaving just a film a brush
would scour and somewhere else perhaps a name
a manifest preserves, no more, soiled paper,

an entry of the People of the Book,
no more. My faith would be no matter, then.
That Florentine who found a place for Jews
in heaven, found his faith's firm proof in spirit

discerned by him to flow from testaments
both old and new, that proved itself (he thought)
by turning the world Christian. Sorry sight.
Where Canaan wept, then Jews wept for their mercy.

Perhaps only a god could limn the world
so like as it is set in Torah: YHWH
(as we transliterate the name who've lost
the way to shape in breath its living vowels)

if I could see the hand that held the pen
at work in what the pen describes, and not
mere words so faithful to the facts they match,
I'd grant to You this life I hold so barely.

3

I do not seek to strike a bargain. Who
is there to bargain with? Who'd dicker with
his life? Not even David at his lyre
sought more than explanation or assurance.

Child of my time, I pose my hopeful wish
in terms not distant from the elegant
brutality we put to nature in
our science: Show me what to build belief of.

Such questions beggar god, whose residence
is what we do not know. All consciousness,
a "neural darwinist" explains, derives
from shapes the brain cells grow to form their web and

the strength each gains to send its news and goods
across each synapse, wide as Hellespont:
at some, whole fleets of ferries haul freight trucks,
pedestrians and cars; at others, beached, its

oars grey and feathered, oarlocks red with rust,
a dinghy collects rain. And "*qualia*,"
"beyond all explanation," he terms what
the poem carries from the lonely confines

of one poor Yorick to another, lost
to scientific reason because fleet
beyond all capture and unique; but here
and undeniable the dinghy shifts as

you settle on its battered bench and press
it deeper, gliding through encircling fog,
the vividly corroded, creaking pins
twin fulcra of your seeming gainless motion

around which you, off center, pull and gasp
and sense, although you cannot say, just what
this boat is that you ride, and what the cool,
uncolored medium your oars kick swirls in.

4

When Dante, having trekked at reason's heels
through hell, arrived in paradise and left
that guide behind, he did not find at first
the woman who would take him on to heaven.

Instead he walked a while beside a stream
with someone whose benignity no doubt
could question, though a stranger. Perhaps I, too,
am wandering an interval consigned to

the love of one I hardly know until
I am delivered over to that state
beyond our need for oxygen. That one
could be myself. In my sole company, on

unsteady feet last summer wading in
a rocky-bottomed river, waters red
as tea that spilled through spindly pines packed dense
as felt, I flicked my bright green line and landed

my feathered hook with grace to drift in sync
among the other floating bugs and bits
of forest this and that right over where
there were no fish, and never have felt closer

in life so far to something that could be
acceptance of existence wholly bound
to matter *or* suffused with deity,
suspended between both in pressing currents.

As it is written, god, when queried, said
that we may tell the true from false among
those claiming prophecy to be their gift
by seeing what among the things predicted

has come to pass. Empirical, this test:
when no vibration, fast or slow, that quakes
on my tympanic membrane can be heard,
with me a theory will have found, at last, rest.

Artwork by Cecilia Soprano

Where God Lives
Robens Napolitan

I remember folding my child fingers
into play church steeples
and then shaping them into strange animal heads
in the jeweled sunlight that streamed
through the windows of my father's church.
My mother didn't seem to mind
as long as I was quiet.

In my palms, the heat of suppressed youth pulsed
and ran up past the restricting cuffs
of my Sunday dress into my restless arms.
I ached to open them, embrace everything,
and dance up and down the church aisles
shouting the new swear words
that I'd learned secretly
from my older brother and his friends.

Like tenuous spider webs, the lines of opportunity
marked my palms with things to come.
I pondered them silently throughout the labored singing
of hymns about Almighty God in off-key voices.
After church, I escaped to the orchard,
laid on my back in the tall grass,
and tracked the clouds that raced overhead.
I counted them until I ran out of numbers.
I watched too how a winter-dried tansy head swayed
under the weight of a red-winged blackbird
as he sang his hymn from the orchard's edge.

Today the wind blows out of the southwest,
miles off the ocean and still coming.
The mountains between there and here have freshened it,
taken out the salt and moisture, leaving just the clouds.
They pause overhead on their way to Montana
so that I can again count them.
I stretch my arms wide, open my hands
and feel the wind lick each finger.
As the wind blows my hair against my cheek
I lean into it, remembering
the first time I realized where God lives.

Right after Mass
Len Roberts

Plastic crucifixes
  glinted
from the rusted fence
as she bent to twist
white bandages around
limp tomato plants,
lay the mulch with
  a *Satan begone*
intoned just as she did
at high mass, the spray
of her hand and flick
of wrist the same
as when the holy oil
  spattered
our young faces
looking up at her
  passing,
the priest's helper,
God's aid who would
  cross
herself all the way
up Ontario Street
and down Olmstead
until she could kneel
in the chrism-blessed dirt
of her own backyard
and tap the seeds
in with the Holy Spirit
  still upon her,
wings spread wide
in that morning light
  as I
balanced on the fence
to watch her separate
the evil from the good,
The wheat from the chaff

as she'd whisper it,
reminding me my mother
would still probably
be at Boney's Bar
sleeping it off,
that my father's piss-
stained sheets hung
like flags of sin
just four yards down,
telling me as she rose
on dirt-crusted knees
that I, too, would be
turned into a swine
and driven off
some high cliff
if I did not heed
  the mark
God had branded me with,
her thick hands grasping
the splotched shape
of purple wings outspread
across the back of my neck
that even then were lifting me up.

Silent Night

Anya Krugovoy

Christmas Eve, my mother and sister and I stand
In the darkened church, making ourselves a tight row,
And each year, I find myself unable to sing
The words that we always save for this night.

It's not just the dead who leave their silent
Footfalls on the stone, or the living faces around me
Growing older and silvered, year after year falling away
Like buttons from their sleeves.

It might be the other things we've lost:
The deep snows I remember from my childhood
In winters now strangely warm and wet,
The paper windows we opened one by one,
Peering into their opalescent, secret worlds.

Or it might just be the notes that linger and shine in the candle-
Gilded air on this winter night that celebrates life and birth,
The notes carrying us through the cold air and the earth
To the dark breast of the mother, reminding us of sleep,
Of calm, of everything we desire and lose and hope to recover
That's peaceful, and tender, and mild.

Vision at the Edge of the Forest *by Mihai Ursachi*
translated by Adam J. Sorkin

O Lord, the night sky burst open in thunder and rain,
and in the splendor of brightness there descended to me
a terrifying dragon with plumes of airy gold.
And like a stone, I stood stone-still by the wall of the forest.
He had soft hair white as snowdrifts,
he appeared right before me: "Behold, I am the Basilisk,
the Good. Make thyself ready!"—and like stone I stood stone-still
by the wall of the forest of stone.

    ...Later, summer showers fell throughout the forest,
    and the acacias scattered flowers, holy and white,
    filling the purple traces of his footsteps...

In the Land of Gilead *by Mihai Ursachi*
translated by Adam J. Sorkin

A threefold rose I picked in the Land of Gilead:
the white is death, the red is life,
and the mourning rose—the empire of the abyss.

Spring Narrative *by Mihai Ursachi*
Translated by Adam J. Sorkin and Doru Motz

Without fear, without hope, I shall tell
the tale. Exactly what was, and
how it took place.

The child was dressed in red velvet,
his features fair, his hair in curls,
his eyes like an early-morning flax flower. He wore
a white lace collar, and in his hand he held some kind of wand,
a thin stick gleaming like platinum. A sharp point.
He was in an endless vineyard, wandering
among the arcana of the wild vines' tendrils,
which were in bloom. (The flower
was like honey, intoxicating, ravishing.)

Along the vines drunk with flowers,
simple snails climbed meekly. They were millions, millions
under the glad sky, in the golden vineyard.
The buzz of insects, the angels. Such peace.

The child has chosen one of the snails. (There were millions.)
It was climbing with care, with hope, along a flowering vine.
This is the one the child had chosen.
(In the crystalline air, angels, their voices
translating destiny, hovering in whispers.)

With the sharp point, the boy touched the little horns. And the snail drew in its tentacles.
Next, its yellow body—a hypothesis of life.
The snail retracted into the shell. Then dropped to the earth.

With his thin metal rod, the child followed after, into the shell.
Deeper, ever deeper. This went on for thousands of years. Until
there was no life, none left at all. Then
the child declared, "I know you. I love you.
I know you."

(Hovering in the crystalline air, angels, their serene voices
translating destiny.)

This is the story called
"The Child with a Snail in a Wand."
This is how it took place.

At Meeting: "Where is the divine tragedy?"
Toria Angelyn Clark

"Seal sports in the spray-whited
circles of cliff-wash."
—Ezra Pound

Cinereal (List of Gray)

Dove, felt, slush, silver
    Sky, hills, granite, wave
        Sweatshirt, gunbarrel, hair
    Pearl, heather, please, powder

        Ash, elephant, seal, air
      Distinguished, noble, dusk, doleful
    Waxpale, mouse, melancholy, sword
      Welkin (vault of heaven)

      Steel, slate, grease, grovel
        Gravel, gravestone, pencil, tin
          Quaker, earth, death, cuff and
        Collar, prison, pebble, chalk
          Hook, wool, smoke, gloom, tomb, rain

God

Scott Struman

Friday night
in Grand Rapids,
Sarah says
"I do everything
in my life knowing
there is a God."

Saturday night
at the wedding,
I wonder as I watch
the Jewish newlyweds dancing,
surrounded by family and friends—
who put the spark
in their lives
to make them so happy
if not God?

The next morning
I drive on Highway 96
to Ann Arbor.
On the road,
the fresh carcasses
of opossums and raccoons
and upside-down turtles
litter my lane
in a bloody,
zig-zag path.

On Moving into the Hollow Square
Deborah Robson

Silence fills the room first. This ordinary space occupies the second floor of an old building adjacent to a public outdoor swimming pool, which is drained and covered in blue tarps because this is November. Early on a quiet Saturday morning, a swish-slide of footsteps comes up the building's stairs, directly from the outside to the upper level. The thumb-latch clicks and, as the heavy door swings open, the air pressure inside the large space shifts with a sigh. One pair of leather-soled shoes taps across the wooden floor, the sound bouncing back from the sheetrock ceilings and walls.

With a clunk, a steel folding chair leaves the rolling storage rack at the end of the room, and its feet hit the floor with staccato clangs. The shoes cross the room and back, and a second chair rattles to its open position and thunks into place next to the first. Another person arrives, and the almost inaudible squeak of rubber soles syncopates with the original set of footsteps. The speed of the chairs' placement increases, making the almost-rhythmic pattern more complex.

When the arrangement is complete, all the chairs face the open center of a hollow square. The front row on each side contains about six seats. One or two additional rows of chairs line up directly behind each front row. The goal is to have enough seats, without many extra spaces. The square needs to be as tight as possible.

Shape note, also called *sacred harp* or *fasola*, is a form of *a cappella* or purely vocal, music, without instrumental accompaniment. One alternate name for the tradition, *sacred harp*, may refer to each singer's vocal cords or to the effect created by the singers' combined voices.

The tradition developed in New England and then moved to, and grew even stronger in, Southern communities. Solidly rural through most of its history, shape note now forms the nucleus of urban gatherings as well and has moved back north. Large singings occur today in small churches in Alabama and Georgia, as they have for many years. Regular groups of singers also gather in northern cities like Boston, Minneapolis, Chicago, Seattle.

Many of the lyrics reflect a historic Christian theology and the larger gatherings open and close with prayers, but the music and its practice remain fiercely nondenominational. When singers gather, no one talks about religion.

The door at the top of the stairs is propped open and more people begin to arrive. Shape note involves four-part harmony, and the singers of each part sit on one side of the square in a prescribed arrangement. A tenor drops his songbook in the second row of the section of chairs closest to the entrance and then eases between the seats to chat with a friend he hasn't seen in months. The location of the tenors, whose part carries the primary melody, determines the positions of the other parts. Another tenor, very experienced, sets her book on a chair in the front row of the same section. As a front-row singer, she will assume extra, unspoken responsibility for the progress of the day's singing.

Altos, mostly women, take chairs in the section that looks toward the door. Trebles, the men and women who will sing the high harmony, gather in the section to the tenors' right, and the basses, mostly men, sit on the tenors' left. One after another, people thump thick books on the seats to claim places, and then slide canvas bags containing throat lozenges and piles of loose papers underneath their chairs. Beginners hover at the back, able to perceive that order exists but not able to determine their places in it. Although the locations for the parts seem arbitrary, old-time singers politely direct or redirect newcomers while making sure everyone has a songbook. There's a cardboard box full of extras, for short- or long-term loan.

Much of what constitutes shape-note singing continues through oral tradition and its fine points have to be learned from other singers, not a book. There are no rehearsals, and there is no audience. A good voice is not required. To a nonparticipating listener, the music comes across as an almost strident sort of cacophony, with several strongly defined melodic lines bursting against each other. On field recordings from the collections of the Smithsonian or the Library of Congress, shape note sounds like barely organized vocal tumult.

Although the arrangement of parts within the room is predetermined, anybody can sing any part at any time by changing positions. Beginners tend to focus on a single part. Some experienced singers join in where they are needed most.

The tenors carry the recognizable tune, but the other parts are not subservient. They don't just dress up the melody. They command independent character. Also, the chords in shape note often leave out the blending tones, or they substitute slightly dissonant notes. The results sound a bit strange.

There are two volumes: loud and loudest, with only a handful of quiet exceptions. Almost always, louder is better. Tempos can be rapid or stately, or can alternate from one to the other, leaving new singers scrambling to figure out why the pace suddenly shifted to double-time.

Singers pick up their books and take their seats around the square. The chairs rattle against the floor, then become quiet as the singers' bodies settle in to fix them securely in place. There's a trick to holding this cumbersome book, a burgundy hardcover of nearly six hundred pages called The Sacred Harp. *Bound along one of its short sides, it opens to a substantial width. If you try to manage it with one hand on each wing, the book's own weight tries to pull it closed. Besides, you need your right hand free to mark time and to turn pages. Rest its left half along your left forearm, and use the widely splayed fingers of your left hand to brace its right half.*

Shape note is a living tradition. New songs constantly join the repertoire. Between revisions of *The Sacred Harp*, singers' bags bulge with photocopied pages of works-in-progress or treasures from other gatherings, other songbooks. Songs travel between groups as singers charter buses or catch low-fare plane tickets to attend weekends of singing far from their homes. Local singers provide food, shelter for those who need it, and the best singing space they can find. That space rarely exists in a modern sanctuary. Carpeting deadens the sound.

You balance the unwieldy book and someone calls a song by its page number, not its name. Long-time singers know the names that go with the numbers. As soon as "Eighty-four" is called, the tune to "Amsterdam" begins to go through their heads. "One-eighty-nine on-the-bottom" translates to "Montgomery." Many tunes carry the names of places important to the composers, names that have nothing to do with the lyrics or tune.

Pages rustle as singers hurry to find the selection. Everyone wants to sing as many songs as possible in the allotted time. The person who chose this song stands up and moves to the center of the square, where the sounds of the four parts will join most tumultuously and most perfectly.

An experienced person in the front of the tenor section selects a key based on the ranges of the singers present, not the printed notes, and quickly vocalizes selected pitches within that key. At least one singer in each other part quickly grabs that group's first note from the air and hums it. Others lean in to check their pitches against this reference point.

Pitching starts while people are looking for the right page, and singing begins as soon as most people have located the song.

At a convention or other large gathering, the person who pitches always gets the key right on the first try, and the song starts immediately. In smaller groups, in which singers are learning to pitch, a few people in each part take the initial pitch as a suggestion, then swiftly read ahead in the music and check how high or low they'll need to go as the song proceeds. Sometimes the pitch is adjusted up or down in a democratic matter of seconds.

The first singing of a tune goes "by the shapes." The notes on the songbook's pages are not the familiar ovals but are squares, circles, triangles, and a sprinkling of diamonds. Originally devised as a teaching aid for sight-singing, these shapes relate to the scale relationships within the song, not to the key in which it is written.

On this first singing—at full volume and full speed—each part sings its own shapes and therefore different syllables. A clattering of *fa*, *sol*, *la*, and *mi* comes from all sides, sometimes accompanying wildly dissonant harmonies, sometimes sliding into sweet resolution. Newcomers sing *la*, *la*, *la*. On really fast passages, more people sing *la*, *la*, *la*. The most proficient singers hit the correct syllabic sound every time and can sight-read new music without a slip.

By custom, after the first run-through, the singers shift without pause from shapes to the words of the verses.

The singing becomes a whole-body experience as singers around the room move their free right arms up and down with the beat, up and down, up and down, pushing the notes out and staying together, singing together, loudly striking both harmony and dissonance with conviction. Long-time singers hold their books open in front of them, eyes closed, arms moving up and down, feeling the music from the soles of their feet to the tops of their heads, surrounded by the living sound reflected back from the other voices and by the room itself, which comes alive, sheltering the square.

At small gatherings, each person chooses a song in turn, and the circuit around the room repeats until the singing time ends. At larger conventions, people's names are put on index cards. Each person selects one song at a time. Sometimes the person who calls a song is five years old, sometimes eighty-five. The person may have been singing for decades, or since yesterday. You can pick a song by opening the book at random, if you like; when you ponder your choice for too long, other singers may suggest the numbers of their favorites. The only thing you can't do is call a song that's already been sung by this group in this session. No repeats: There are too many great songs, and there's too little time.

You can learn a lot about the shape-note experience by singing from your part's side, but there's nothing like the hollow within the square. The time comes when you've got to move to the middle. You can ask another person to stand there with you, or you can look straight at the front-row tenors with "help" in your eyes, but whatever you need, the group will give you. And in return it's best if you can pick a song you care about because this is a gift you give to yourself and to the group around you.

Will it be 452 on-the-bottom, the second song on that page, "Martin," the one that heals your soul when you're so tired of life you think you can't go on? Some years, you call "Martin" at every singing. Or maybe 154, less cathartic, but still reassuring that *There is rest for the weary, there is rest for you.* Perhaps 497, "Natick," whose chorus soars: *Sweet Redeemer, from above, born on wings, on wings of love....* Or doleful 47 on-the-bottom, "Idumea," *And am I born to die? To lay this body down! And must my trembling spirit fly into a world unknown?*

As your gift to the other singers, you bring your passion and need for a particular piece of music. Each time, they give the song back to you in a way you've never known before.

So you consider which song you will call as you clutch the book with its hundreds of tested compositions or you grasp the awkward pages of a new song, and your neighbor takes a turn, chooses a song, and the four parts sight-read it loud and fast, and when they nail the harmonies, a bit of the universe clicks into place like the tumblers of a lock lining up before the door swings open. Even though the harmonies sometimes come together and sometimes drift around the edges as less-experienced singers learn on the fly, this isn't practice; it's the real thing, the living music, the union of voices, not trained but proficient and confident, as those with more experience carry those who sit at the edges of the square until one of the new ones catches a running phrase in the treble or an alto's fuguing entrance just right and the feeling hits a place deep within, a place the new singer had forgotten was there in the midst of everyday life, and one more person is hooked.

The long-time singers nearby clearly have heard this change in tone, but they don't react much—they're too caught in the music themselves—yet John in the bass section almost smiles, and Mary Lou with the altos sings even more strongly, and the arms around the square move vigorously up and down, following the person who called the song and following the front-row singers, the strongest singers, and another voice has just become a string in the sacred harp, here, now.

And the tempest grows bigger and it's a profound experience even if you don't share your neighbor's beliefs, whatever they are, and you're singing Our bondage it shall end, by and by, *or* Jesus, lover of my soul, *even if you've never found a creed you could honestly recite, but there's a power in this room that does love your soul, and your soul loves it back, so you keep returning to take your place on one side of the square, to pull your book from the canvas bag that says* Rocky Mountain Sacred Harp Convention, *the bag itself signed in permanent marker by a bunch of the folks you've sung with, some from here and some from Georgia and some from places you might never see, and your book's binding has been mended with red duct tape that is far brighter than the original burgundy, and you stand up and walk forward, clearly calling "One fifty-nine"—a beginner's song to select, but there's no song like it, and no better way to sing it than this, and the old-timers are glad there's someone new here to call it—because you need to choose the songs that mean the most to you, the ones you want to have surround you and lift you up, and you step into the middle of the square and wave your arm up and down, hoping you're doing it right, but the front-row tenors always have it right and the rest of the group has one eye on them and one eye on you, and it's your song, so they look to you for the signals about where to skip the repeats, and which verses to do, all of which you're letting them know by holding up your fingers or beating harder with one arm to keep the song rolling into a repeat, and the massive book lies open along your other arm, its spine nestled into the pulse-point at your wrist, even though you don't need to look at this song any more because it's in your blood, in your bones, deeper than a sigh, so you sing with your eyes half-closed, watching the tenors through your eyelashes, slightly out of focus, as they slide the melody cleanly in and out between the other parts, then you slowly revolve within the space and keep turning, to glory in the trebles' strong, high notes, the altos' subtle trills through the center, the basses' vital rumble, all tumbling together, and, singing loudly yourself, you receive the sound in a torrent as the four sides of "Wondrous Love" cascade toward you, and it's all happening now, right at the center of your body, the center of your mind, the center of your soul, in the center of the square.*

thunderstorm spiritual
Christopher Luna

the last drops of rain pick out a tune
caught by leaves in gospel succession
one moment jazz thrash the next
front porches
     secure canopies
        sacred spaces
offer safe distance from storm
viewed through waterfall veil
eyes closed   as lips mouth most solemn vow
surrender to cycle of precipitation
barely awake   yet recognize
that all timing   even bad timing
is on time   by design
and all that is split
must one day
reconverge

Tracks of Sound and Water
Cynthia Hogue

a fairytale for Hannah

A boy spends seven years painting clouds,
learning to read what they tell.
Finally, his paintings become sky.

> Here, a mist of sulfur
> rises off the bay.
> No trees to hide me
> from the distant glacier,
> the salmon sun
> singeing horizon, the wind burning.

He spends seven years learning the uses
of plants—eucalyptus, chamomile, nettle—
names that he can hear the wind in,
as when he gathered them
from hills, desert, and woods.

Seven years healing
until he's alert
as a deer in open field.
Always he's preparing
for a dream someone else would have.

> How long did I look,
> at last calling myself back?
> Through amber fumes steeping up,
> the bay smoking, mountains in clouds.

An eagle tries to catch a dolphin
for so many years he understands at last
the creature's laughing.
The dreamer says, *When you hear that
from one in human form
you'll see cloud leaf root water—
as sound—and the joy in that
will fool you.*

I heard chants.
Five times at the mountain's foot
near the corpse-stones,
I was dipped in the well,
once for each note of the scale.

The dreamer's eyes narrow
until the boy sees only
black pupil, is thrown
to the ground.
There are three tasks left.
The first is to discover the other two.
When you know the second,
become the third.

I knew I was a dream as well,
not looking, through fine mist,
but there, with the wings
I had need of.

A raven starts from the bush,
flies up cawing.
The sound stays with the boy's body for years.
The dreamer says, *I leave you with this:*
When you've fulfilled the last,
it is fire, not air,
you'll gather.

Where is there left to look?
And this evening, when the wind dies
and the sun drops from the clouds ...

The boy cannot tell whether it's song
or the peal of laughter around and inside him.
The sound becomes a trail
he follows to the water's edge,
wades in, then swims out—
at times leaping airborn—
into the flickering tracks of light.

Large Bodies of Water
Carolyn Dille

Smell
is
one
molecule
of pine
one
of dust
taste
a crystal
of salt
inner
and outer
ears
hear
the same sound
water and skin and air
a single atmosphere

the cushion
of algae
and history
rearranges
the common
senses
the mantle
that shields
shrouds
us
is a veil
of light
at the eye's horizon

Rain
Elizabeth Howard

Take care, my daily words.
As you step forth,
the hillock erupts,
settles slow motion
to a dusty sinkhole.
I would gather you up
if I knew to go east.
Or west. Where is your foot,
all those marathon marches
for freedom? Hand, shaped
to the plow, tilling grain
to feed the people?
Sweet words scattered
on the searing wind,
thunder closing us in.
Surrounded,
         red wings
           and petals
             falling,
I sink to the earth,
dribble down the furrow
like a clod of loam
in winter rain.

Less
Barbara Daniels

She can be happy with bare days, thinned blood,
repetition of rain on narrow streets, a heavy sweater.

In the Blackwood graveyard, a hawk-headed god
presses a carved door that never opens.

Color washed from him to white and gray.
Flowers brown in heaps by the gravestones.

She reaches in to straighten plastic carnations.
Plastic lasts, a refuge of color. She doesn't have much

to complain of—lost church services, warm crayons,
raw macaroni pasted on construction paper

to form arabesques and Bible verses.
Secretly she broke off hard elbows and ate them,

consuming the unbending Word. Now she pulls up
her collar, stuffs fists into her pockets.

She likes graveyards when they're full of strangers.
She imagines she'll continue, durable and serious as bone.

Fossils
Emory Elkins

A gray day to end
all gray days. And all the transients are out,
passing through, seeming to be quite busy
adjusting umbrellas, cursing smokestacks, straightening slumped shoulders,
mumbling about the chemicals in the air.

This mist must be the swamp's advantage—although we've had our share
of dirty-faced bastards here, beating themselves with lunch-pails;
there have been no drunken fisticuffs between street-corners lately—
perhaps the occasional dealer, with the dancing crack pipe,
followed by several stumbling fools — but they never speak;
I stay obsessed with facts.

Lately I've been too busy—blowing up balloons
and sending them off to heaven—to give a good goddamn.
The release of effluvium
makes all things much nicer: the getting used to it,
the getting on with it, ignoring familiar strangers,
inhaling microcosmic particulars, picking the gum from my shoe.
Still, sometimes I get scared.

When I see my friend Moses, he reassures me,
neither of us are dead—lately though he tells me
that he thinks he's a snail. That's ok.
We're breathing.

Sacrifice

Atticus James Tolan

At the factory, where people
watch machines press dough
into unleavened biscuits
the size of a Roman coin,
there is one whose
family has been saving
their communion wafers
for years, holding them
in their mouths until
safely back at the pew,
where they seal them in Baggies
each will smuggle home
in hopes of piecing together
the mystery of their lord's body
on a cross laid out in the garage.

Resurrection
Aliki Barnstone

I took my body with me
and waved goodbye to the angels in my tomb
who sat where my head and feet had been.
I am everywhere alive, a word,
my blood the happy red tulips,
my eyes new leaves blinking in the sun.
I am flesh among you and I am lonely
walking the yellow highway lines,
carrying four brown paper bags
full of newspapers, the sins of the world,
my hair lighted, a halo of mercury
in a candelabra of streetlights.
I leave my footprints to shine, oil on asphalt.
I have a body so I dream of Mary
washing my feet with her tears
and drying them with her hair.
I smell myrrh, remember her anointing fingers,
my cock rising toward paradise.
I am everywhere and I am inside her,
lost in balms, my eyes blazing
as my skin becomes hers,
and I am she,
a woman, flesh and blood, blessing the union.

Questions
Peter E. Murphy

The truth comes out when the spirit goes in.
—Irish proverb

My tongue rubs itself
against the resonance
of abstract words
whose syllables nudge
the flesh and bones
of consciousness
to pronounce
the unknowable.
A sun whose light
dazzles so we only see
this world where want is.
You call it a leap,
and I agree, like
the imagination that spells
the truth of poems.
Evil is a turning away,
suffering intended
so our bodies learn to trudge
on knees and elbows,
while our faces facing
the earth lift like heliotropes
toward the awesome.

My name is Peter, petros, rock—
a lexicon of doubt
and betrayal, a fashioning
of molecules beaten
by invisible gusts that raze
my sandstone face
from the rough host
of its body and send it
swirling into the source
of the sky. I can't see it,
good friend, but I know
it's there.

for Stephen Dunn

Woman Dies in Rural Crash
Karen Craigo

This morning as mud anchored me
in corn stubble, I held a broken woman
in my viewfinder, autofocus humming
in my hands. I circled her car to show impact,
proximity, the muscular work of rescuers.
Maybe it's true our last seconds happen
in slow motion, and time had not resumed
its measured ticking as I lifted my shoes
from the firmament, left, right, then left again.
With the rain, it may be weeks before Joe Potter
plants the wheat seed piled in his outbuilding
and commerce supersedes this town's sorrow.
Crop rotation and the seasons ensure that his field
will look different by April, that it will not appear
this way again to anyone but the woman
who found her there, or the volunteer firefighter
who felt the last drumming of her pulse,
or me, apart and silent, a bystander. Tonight
her father will open his newspaper;
he will wear the wonder and sorrow he once saw
on the face of a child as her balloon was stolen
by the wind. He will imagine I felt something less
than sadness as her soul emerged from its casing,
something other than amazement at how life spills
from a body like water from a clay pot. We all
have to die, and that is something we say out loud,
over and over, thinking we believe because proof
is newsprint staining our fingers. When I go,
I want to imagine there is someone, solemn
in a field or silent at home—someone, rooted
here, whose prayers will follow me upward.

White Light Work
Ken Waldman

First, take the white light
of spirit to heart. Sparkled blood will
renew the body by night

as you dream your usual dream: bright
far stars above a bright far hill.
Next, take the white light

of that hill to bone, an icy climb into fright.
But what a view. The glimpse of heaven will
renew the body by night,

the star-filled sky a black kite
of diamonds, dark air perfectly still.
Next, take the white light

of those stars to mouth, and bite.
Swallow, then blow. Dazzling breath will
renew the body by night

as steady puffs of love take flight
in your soul, sailing you downhill
at last. Take the white light.
Renew the body by night.

Sunlit Interrogation
Judith Pordon

In an empty lot
with motors, tires,
a congregation of tired feet,

beside bougainvilla
and a once a week watered palm,
a lone chair waits.

Sink into white
plastic. Balance heels
on brazen cement.

Your shadow
will hint
of right or wrong.

Look closely.
Your sermon
is underfoot.

Resolution
Beth Partin

Let there be light happened just this gradually,
not like flipping a switch
in the bathroom on Monday morning.
Stars contradanced as the sun
dallied on the other side
of the earth. All the while the moon
coming into its shape of light—

December solstice conjunct full moon:
from now on the sky lit longer
and longer by the sun, impossible
to observe like the face of God.
But the moon like a mirror
invites the human gaze,
like God's watch-face tells
no time but tides, like a silent
oracle offers no prophecies
too encrypted for a sleepy
woman in her kitchen
delaying sunrise
with her eyes.

To a Friend Nursing
a Beyond Death Experience
Richard Alan Bunch

Horizons are bandits, you say,
Resting half mad in the eastern rain,
That we here are dreamers of fury,
Victims of copper angst,
Thighs of our vulnerable maybes.

The certitude in your voice and your gait
Concerns me.
You say roofless silence,
That swallow of the summits,
Carries the day, that there's no fear in journeys
Of the spirit,
Manifestos of the sun,
In putting out, in the last of earth,
That there's more beauty in the laughter
Waking over there.

It is not for me to parade,
Sometimes in unwitting dress,
Upon your solitudes, the heart of your reach
Of constant fire
Those sprinkling sands of staging a comeback.
I have my own paradoxes to live,
My pangs, with all their wintry diamonds, to die.

As It Happens
Mark Irwin

those two people are setting off invisible sparks. They
are moving toward a greater fire, one beyond that of green
and flowers blossoming. And the light, handling the moment,
is undoing itself, not moving, but surrounding, becoming
all things. As it happens these two people are part of the present's
breathtaking picture, a picture that's shattered over and over, pumping
a long blush upon other people, places.
As it happens there are many sparks that grow
into greater points of light, distant, skeletal, constellating
beyond like the tiny gears of an even greater, invisible
flower where the remembered and unremembered float
like bees. As it happens we are not here long, so we must
choose words that will slowly melt, illumining dark corners
of the world, and remain—faint tracings—in what decays.

Capillary Attraction
G. C. Waldrep

Drop of blood, pin's prick
so perfect, the flattening of gravity
imperceptible as it rests
at skin's surface. What I want
is wholeness, completion,
the chain of being—sweet myth—
reforged, and more light,
the kind that pours like clear
river water, tumbling over stones,
filling the small places
with the clatter of its industry.
In short: the machine in the garden,
stacked pyramids of hay,
threshing crew resting
in the photographer's exposure,
leaning on steel, arms crossed
against all easy polities.
They look serious. Behind them
the sky is clear, no hint of storm,
of clouds or of the sudden
wind that can pierce clapboard
with a straw's shaft. Somewhere
they have supper waiting,
drink, a bed, perhaps a woman's touch
light as the smear of blood
on my forearm. We are ghosts
to them, dwelling on the outskirts
as we do: heart's murmur,
desire's heavy pulse.

Western Exposure
Joyanna Laughlin

The Universe has a G spot
but it never stays in one place
it is everywhere
at the speed of light

On a mesa in New Mexico
thinking of Roswell, UFOs, sunsets
the earth in this place strips me
raw enough to feel just a little
of how big the Universe really is and
the click of each world fitting into place

Night and the stars come too close
without buildings, without walls
those worlds are too close
somebody might really be out there
I could scream without walls
and the sky is blue not black
where the moon bleeds
into it

I walkabout,
listen to the moonlight
smell the rain
taste the wind through piñon pines
do not see the fledgling owl in my path
until he's lighting up my blind side
right in front of me,
we stare at each other for awhile
he's curious, so am I
sand scatters as he mantles
white feathers, gray flecks, silent departure

Day comes
and the high desert clouds
trail gray shadows over sharp peaks
then dark wooded triangles
like a fringed shawl catching no threads

Gethsemane
Lois Marie Harrod

At night the blossoms
we thought
food for stars

neither mingle
nor hiss
as they fall

open
into the shut fist
of the sun.

My father
said he understood
why rain

could not order
the moon
to dismiss

the persistent
suffering
of sand.

I do not think
he said much
he could regret.

But for this, his
silence,
a sweaty stone.

More I could tell you,
and the dark role
of the absent landlord

would become evident
in the tragic hall
of goats.

I was supposed
to be a boy
named Paul.

I do not ask you
to make sense
of the universe

only to watch
with me again
a little while.

Evangelical

Steve Langan

Because it has always been it shall remain thus,
sanctification just part of the ongoing episode
about the loss of faith,
which suggests it will involve tears and scarves,
scarred retinas, dangling corneas,
and statuary the housekeeper dusts with a flower.

We hope this does not frighten you much,
escorting you into the unlocked chambers.
Let me assure you we have spent many hours strolling.
Your hand is cold. This is normal.
To your right is a dream; to your left, a mirage.
Your eyes seem troubled. We expect this.

Have you ever despised yourself over the cause
of a riddle? Or started in the middle?
Let me assure you we dream disunion and regret.
And I intended to tell you a host of anecdotes—
but I must return to staring from this misbegotten porch
at the steel sections and long and short tubing

the factory next door has assembled, thinking of the future.
If you wish, we will begin again later.

Abstraction
Anne Coray

And what has word to do with this—a canvas of sky
I cannot bear to put a mark upon? The color is already spoken,
cerulean and still. Nothing the wise need interpret. The paint
that hardens on the sable could have been anything:
apple, grape, or the blood of any fruit. A line, a crucifixion.
Picture, if you will, just this: the testament of the yield of silence.

Abel's Sacrifice
Bea Opengart

He bound the struggling lamb,
stabbed it as if the wound were his own
and the cutting brought him peace:
the body undone,
intimate memory freed
in blood over fist-shaped stones,
boulders pulled from the hillside
where sheep lipped air
as if the manna fell
even then from heaven
anchored by sand
in pillars, held upright
by wind. They were not to be
closed within walls, not climbed
except by a boy who killed
what loved him and set it on fire.
He remembered the tongue on his skin,
forehead against his thigh,
then raised his arm,
preparing.

El Paso del Retorno
Vincente Huidobro

A Raquel que me dijo
un día cuando tú te
alejas un solo instante,
el tiempo y yo lloramos.

Yo soy ese que salió hace un año de su tierra
Buscando lejanías de vida y muerte
Su propio corazón y el corazón del mundo
Cuando el viento silbaba entrañas
En un crepúsculo gigante y sin recuerdos

Guiado por mi estrella
Con el pecho vacío
Y los ojos clavados en la altura
Salí hacia mi destino

Oh mis buenos amigos
¿Me habéis reconocido?
He vivido una vida que no puede vivirse
Pero tú, Poesía, no me has abandonado un solo instante
Oh mis amigos aquí estoy
Vosotros sabéis acaso lo que yo era
Pero nadie sabe lo que soy

El viento me hizo viento
La sombra me hizo sombra
El horizonte me hizo horizonte preparado a todo
La tarde me hizo tarde
Y el alba me hizo alba para cantar de nuevo

Oh poeta, esos tremendos ojos
Ese andar de alma de acero y de bondad de mármol.
Este es aquel que llegó final del último camino
Y que vuelve quizás con otro paso.
Hago al andar el ruido de la muerte
Y si mis ojos os dicen
Cuánta vida he vivido y cuánta muerte he muerto
Ellos podrían también deciros
Cuánta vida he muerto y cuánta muerte he vivido

The Return Step *by Vicente Huidobro*
translated by Sherman Souther

To Raquel who told me
a day when you go
away a single moment
time and I cry

I am the one who a year ago left from his land
Looking for far-off places of life and death
His own heart and the heart of the world
When the wind whistled entrails
In a tremendous twilight without memories

Guided by my star
With vacant breast
And eyes fixed on the summit
I left for my destiny

Oh, my good friends
Have you recognized me?
I have lived a life that cannot be lived
But you Poetry have not once abandoned me
Oh my friends I am here
You know perhaps what I was
But nobody knows what I am

The wind made me wind
The shade made me shade
The horizon made me a horizon prepared for everything
The evening made me evening
And dawn made me dawn in order to sing again

Oh poet those enormous eyes
That steel-souled gait of marble's grace
This is what is reached at the end of the farthest road
And one perhaps returns with a different step
On walking I make the sound of death
And if my eyes say to you
How much life I have lived and how much death I have died

¡Oh mis fantasmas! ¡Oh mis queridos espectros!
La noche ha dejado noche en mis cabellos.
¿En dónde estuve? ¿Por dónde he andado?
¿Pero era ausencia aquélla o era mayor presencia?

Cuando las piedras oyen mi paso
Sienten una ternura que les ensancha el alma
Se hacen señas furtivas y hablan bajo:
Allí se acerca el buen amigo
El hombre de las distancias
Que viene fatigado de tanta muerte al hombro
De tanta vida en el pecho
Y busca donde pasar la noche

Heme aquí ante vuestros limpios ojos
Heme aquí vestido de lejantas
Atrás quedaron los negros nubarrones
Los años de tinieblas en el antro olvidado
Traigo un alma lavada por el fuego
Vosotros me llamáis sin saber a quién llamáis
Traigo un cristal sin sombra un corazón que no decae
La imagen de la nada y un rostro que sonríe
Traigo un amor muy parecido al universo
La Poesía me despejó el camino
Ya no hay banalidades en mi vida
¿Quién guió mis pasos de modo tan certero?

Mis ojos dicen a aquellos que cayeron
Disparad contra mí vuestros dardos
Vengad en mí vuestras angustias
Vengad en mí vuestros fracasos
Yo soy invulnerable.
He tomado mi sitio en el cielo como el silencio.

Los siglos de la tierra me caen en los brazos.
Yo soy, amigos, el viajero sin fin
Las alas de la enorme aventura
Batían entre inviernos y veranos…
Mirad cómo suben estrellas en mi alma
Desde que he expulsado las serpientes del tiempo oscurecido

¿Cómo podremos entendernos?
Heme aquí de regreso de donde no se vuelve
Compasión de las olas y piedad de los astros

They will also say to you
How much life I have died and how much death I have lived

Oh my phantoms! Oh, my dear ghosts!
Night left night in my hair
Where was I? From where did I walk?
But was I that absence or larger presence?

When the stones hear my step
They feel affection that expands the soul
They become secret signs and speak softly
There a good friend approaches
A man of distances
Who comes wearied by so much death on his shoulder
By so much life in his breast
Looking for a place to spend the night

I stand here before your clear eyes
I stand here dressed in distances
Behind remain the black thunderclouds
The years of darkness in the grotto forgotten
I bring a soul washed by fire
You call me without knowing whom you call
I bring a crystal with no shade a heart that does not rot
The likeness of nothing and a face that smiles
I bring a love much like the universe
Poetry cleared the road for me
Now there are no banalities in my life
Who guided my steps in so skillful a way?

My eyes say to them that fell
Hurl your darts against me
Enter me your torments
Enter me your failures
I am invulnerable
I have taken my place in the sky like the silence

The centuries of the earth fall into my arms
I am, friends, the endless traveler
The wings of great adventure
Beat between winters and summers
Look how the stars rise in my soul
Since I have driven out the serpents of clouded time

¡Cuánto tiempo perdido! Este es el hombre de las lejanías
El que daba vuelta las páginas de los muertos
Sin tiempo sin espacio sin corazón sin sangre
El que andaba de un lado para otro
Desesperado y solo en las tinieblas
Solo en el vacío
Como un perro que ladra hacia el fondo de un abismo

¡Oh vosotros! ¡Oh mis buenos amigos!
Los que habéis tocado mis manos
¿Qué habéis tocado?
Y vosotros que habéis escuchado mi voz
¿Qué habéis escuchado?
Y los que habéis contemplado mis ojos
¿Qué habéis contemplado?

Lo he perdido todo y todo lo he ganado
Y ni siquiera pido
La parte de la vida que me corresponde
Ni montañas de fuego ni mares cultivados
Es tanto más lo que he ganado que lo que he perdido
Así es el viaje al fin del mundo
Y ésta es la corona de sangre de la gran experiencia
La corona regalo de mi estrella
¿En dónde estuve en dónde estoy?

Los árboles floran, un pájaro canta inconsolable
Decid ¿quién es el muerto?
El viento me solloza ¡Qué inquietudes me has dado!
Algunas flores exclaman:
¿Estás vivo aún?
¿Quién es el muerto entonces?
Las aguas gimen tristemente
¿Quién ha muerto en estas tierras?

Ahora sé lo que soy y lo que era
Conozco la distancia que va del hombre a la verdad
Conozco la palabra que aman los muertos
Este es el que ha llorado el mundo, el que ha llorado resplandores
Las lágrimas se hinchan se dilatan
Y empiezan a girar sobre su eje.
Heme aquí ante vosotros
Cómo podremos entendemos Cómo saber io que decimos

How can we know us?
I stand here returned from where no one turns around
The waves' compassion and respect of the stars
How much time lost! This is the man of distances
He who strolled the pages of the dead
Without time without space without heart without blood
He who walked from one side to the other
Hopeless and alone in the darkness
Alone in the void
Like a dog growling at the bottom of an abyss

Oh you! Oh my good friends!
You who have touched my hands
What have you touched?
And you who have heard my voice
What have you heard?
And you who have studied my eyes
What have you studied?

I have lost it all and all of it I have gained
And I don't even ask
The part of my life that communicates with me
Neither mountains of fire nor cultivated seas
It is all the more what I have gained what I have lost
Such is the trip to the end of the world
And this one is the bloody crown of great experience
The crown gift of my star
Where was I where am I?

The trees cry a bird inconsolably sings
Ask who is the corpse?
The wind sobs to me what restlessness you have caused me!
Some flowers exclaim
You still live?
Who is the corpse then?
The waters moan sadly
Who has died in these lands?

Hay tantos muertos que me llaman
Allí donde la tierra pierde su ruido
Allí donde me esperan mis queridos fantasmas
Mis queridos espectros.
Miradme, os amo tanto, pero soy extranjero
¿Quién salió de su tierra
    sin saber el hondor de su aventura?
Al desplegar las alas
El mismo no sabía qué vuelo era su vuelo.

Vuestro tiempo y vuestro espacio
No son mi espacio ni mi tiempo
¿Quién es el extranjero? ¿Reconocéis su andar?
Es el que vuelve con un sabor de eternidad en la garganta
    con un olor de olvido en los cabellos
    con un sonar de Venas misteriosas
Es este que está llorando el universo
Que sobrepasó la muerte y el rumor de la selva secreta
Soy impalpable ahora como ciertas semillas
Que el viento mismo que las lieva no las siente
Oh Poesía nuestro reino empieza.

Este es aquel que durmió muchas veces
Allí donde hay que estar alerta
Donde las rocas prohiben la palabra
Allí donde se confunde la muerte con el canto del mar
Ahora vengo a saber que fui a buscar las llaves
He aquí las llaves
¿Quién las había perdido?
¿Cuánto tiempo ha que se perdieron?
Nadie encontró las llaves perdidas en el tiempo y en las bruma
¡Cuántos siglos perdidas!
Al fondo de las tumbas
Al fondo do los mares
Al fondo del murmullo de los vientos
Al fondo del silencio
He aquí los signos
¡Cuánto tiempo olvidados!
Pero entonces amigo ¿Qué vas a decirnos?
¿Quién ha de comprenderte? ¿De dónde vienes?
¿En dónde estebas? ¿En qué alturas en qué profundidades?
Andaba por la Historia del brazo con la muerte

Now I know what I am and what I was
I know the distance a man goes for truth
I know the word loved by the dead
This is what the world has cried what splendors have cried
The tears swell up spread
And begin spinning over your eye
I stand here before you
How can we understand us how to know what we say
There are so many dead that call me
There where the earth loses its sound
There where I wait for my dear phantoms
My beloved ghosts
Look at me I love you so much but I am a foreigner
Who left from your land not knowing how profound his adventure?
On spreading wings
He himself did not know which flight was his flight

Your time and your space
They are not my space nor time
Who is the foreigner? Do you recognize his gait?
It is he who returns with the taste of eternity in his throat
            with the smell of oblivion in his hair
            with the sound of mysterious veins
This is what the universe is crying
What overcame death and the whisper of the hidden jungle
I am intangible now like certain seeds
Carried by the same wind that does not feel them
Oh Poetry our kingdom begins

This is who slept often
There where alertness is necessary
Where stones forbid the word
There where death is confused with the song of the sea
Now I know that I went away to look for the keys
I have here the keys
Who would have lost them?
How long ago were they lost?
Nobody found the keys lost in time and the mists
How many centuries lost!
At the bottom of tombs
At the bottom of seas
At the bottom of the winds' sigh

Oh hermano, nada voy a decirte
Cuando hayas tocado lo que nadie puede tocar
Más que al árbol te gustará callar

At the bottom of silence
I have the signs
How much time forgotten!
But now friend what are you about to tell us?
Who must understand you? From where do you come?
Where were you? At what heights and what depths?
You walked through History arm in arm with death

Oh brother I am going to tell you nothing
When you have touched that which no one can touch
More than the tree you will be pleased to silence

Solitario Invencible
Vicente Huidobro

Resblando
Como canasta de amarguras
Con mucho silencio y mucha luz
Dormido de hielos
Te vas y vuelves a ti mismo
Te ríes de tu propio sueño
Pero suspiras poemas temblorosos
Y te convences de alguna esperanza

La ausencia el hambre de callar
De no emitir más tantas hipótesis
De cerrar las heridas habladoras
Te da una ansia especial
Como de nievo y fuego
Quieres volver los ojos a la vida
Tragarte el universo entero
Esos campos de estrellas
Se te van de la mano después de la catástrofe
Cuando el perfume de los claveles
Gira en torno de su eje

Invincible Recluse
By Vicente Huidobro
translated by Sherman Souther

Skidding
Like a basket of bitterness
Filled with silence and light
Frozen asleep
You leave and return to yourself
You laugh at your own dream
Yet you sigh shivering poems
And convince yourself of some hope

Absence, the hunger of keeping silent
Of no longer emitting so many hypotheses
Of closing the talkative wounds
You surrender to a special anxiety
Like from snow and fire
You want to turn your eyes to life
To swallow the entire universe
Those fields of stars
They fly away from your hand after the catastrophe
When the perfume of the carnations
Spins around your axis

Evensong
Todd Davis

Near the gravel pit just below
the crest of Norman Hill, two
fox sprawl, end of day warmth

rising from earth. Across the road,
hay turned into windrows rings
William's field, gold against green

against gold. To the west, sun
lowers itself down the ladder
of the sky, as heavy clouds break

to reveal burnished red of ash
leaves, a fox's tail disappearing
into the undergrowth. At this hour,

what isn't prayer?

About the Contributors

KEITH ABBOTT is working on a novel, *Franklin Furpiece*, chapters of which have been serialized on Andrei Codrescu's Exquisite Corpse website, www.corpse.org. Recent publications include an introduction to Richard Brautigan in the *Edna Webster Collection of Undiscovered Writings*, Houghton Mifflin, 1999. A visual artist, his work has been displayed in a number of galleries, including Indigos Gallery in Denver, Colorado.

ELIZABETH ANDREW is a writing instructor and spiritual director living in Minneapolis, Minnesota. The author of *Swinging on the Garden Gate: A Spiritual Memoir*, she has published essays and short memoirs in both religious and literary journals. She teaches memoir, essay, and journal writing at the Loft Literary Center.

LUCY ARON's work has appeared in newspapers, magazines, anthologies, literary journals, and on-line zines including *Cleveland Plain Dealer*, *Friends Journal*, *Poetry Motel*, *Rockhurst*, *The Bark*, *4X4 The Newport Review*, and *Peregrine*. She is a Buddhist and a Quaker who lives in northern California with her husband, two golden retrievers, and sheep.

DEBORAH BACHARACH is from Seattle, Washington. She has a master's degree in creative writing from the University of Minnesota. Her work has appeared in variety of journals including *Calyx*, *Bridges*, and *Switched-on Gutenburg*. In addition to writing poetry, she practices aikido, a Japanese martial art, and teaches at Highline Community College. She is in the process of submitting her first manuscript, *Welcome to America*.

ALIKI BARNSTONE's recent books of poems are *Wild With It* (The Sheep Meadow Press, 2002) and *Madly in Love* (Carnegie Mellon University Press, 1997). Her poems have recently appeared or will appear in *Agni*, *Antioch Review*, *Boulevard*, *Chicago Review*, *New England Review*, *Ploughshares*, *Southern Review*, *TriQuarterly*, and other journals. She introduced and wrote the readers' notes for *H.D.'s Trilogy* (New Directions, 1998) and is the editor of *A Book of Women Poets from Antiquity to Now* (Schocken/Random House, 1992) and *Voices of Light: Spiritual and Visionary Poems by Women from Around the World* (Shambhala, 1999). She is professor at the University of Nevada, Las Vegas.

WILLIS BARNSTONE is an author, poet, and translator. His latest works are *The New Covenant: Commonly Called The New Testament, The Four Gospels and The Apocalypse* (Penguin Putnam), *The Gnostic Bible* (with Marvin Meyer, Shambhala Publications), and *Life Watch: A Circle of 101 Nights (BOA Editions)*, a book of poems.

DOUG EVANS BETANCO, 56, teaches writing, literature, and globalism at Colorado Mountain College in Glenwood Springs, Colorado. He has spent the last ten years in love with the peasant culture of Northern Nicaragua and with an extended family of Betancos with whom he shares mutual adoptive kinship. He is currently revising a nonfiction novel, *Cristemano!*, about the new-edge interface between First and Third Worlds that transforms both.

LEONARD BORENSTEIN's poems have appeared in a number of journals, most recently *Pivot* and *Neovictorian/Cochlea*. He also has had essays and book reviews published in print and on-line journals, such as *Jewish Review*, *Expansive Poetry* and *Iambs* and *Trochees.com*. On the other side of his creative life, he is a sculptor. In addition to a one-man show, his wood carvings have been included in more than fifty group, juried and invitational shows in the New York area and on the west coast.

MARK BRAZAITIS is the author of *The River of Lost Voices: Stories from Guatemala*, winner of the 1998 Iowa Short Fiction Award, and *Steal My Heart*, a novel published in 2000 by Van Neste Books. His stories, poems, and essays have appeared in *The Sun*, *Beloit Fiction Journal*, *Notre Dame Review*, *Atlanta Review*, and *Shenandoah*. He is an assistant professor of English at West Virginia University.

ANDREA CARTER BROWN's first collection, *Brook & Rainbow*, won the 2000 Sow's Ear Press Chapbook Competition and was published in Spring 2001. Her poems have appeared in *The Gettysburg Review*, *Mississippi Review*, *Marlboro Review*, *Barnabe Mountain Review*, *Borderlands*, and *Phoebe*, among others, and in *Girls: An Anthology* (Global City Press, 1997). A founding editor of the poetry journal *Barrow Street*, her work has won awards from the Poetry Society of America, The Writer's Voice, and the River Oak Review Poetry Prize.

RICHARD ALAN BUNCH was born in Honolulu and grew up in the Napa Valley. His works include *Santa Rosa Plums*, *Wading the Russian River*, and *Sacred Space*. His poetry has appeared in the *Red Cedar Review*, *Haight Ashbury Literary Journal*, *Fugue*, *Long Islander*, *Black Moon*, and the *Hawai'i Review*.

JOAN CANTWELL is an artist and nurse who works as a manager of employee health and wellness for a large Chicago corporation. Joan has been passionate about introducing meditation to employees in her workplace and recently returned from Beijing, where she talked about the positive effects of "Mindfulness Based Meditation in Corporate America." She is a practicing artist with special focus on portraiture and life drawing, is an emerging writer, and had one essay published in *Mediphors*.

CATHY CAPOZZOLI is a poet and author and editor of this special edition of *Many Mountains Moving* as well as a guide entitled *Resources for Creative Writers of the Spiritual*. Her creative works have been published in *Duquesne Magazine*, *Trouble, Beyond Bread,* and the anthology *Voices from the Attic*. She has an M.F.A. in Writing and Poetics from Naropa University in Boulder, Colorado.

DAVID S. CHO teaches composition, creative writing, literature and topics in Asian/American studies as an assistant professor of English at North Park University in Chicago, Illinois, where he resides with his wife Sandy and children Jonathan and Sarah. His work is forthcoming in *American Scholar*, *Prairie Schooner*, and *The Spoon River Poetry Review*, where he is the Illinois Featured Poet.

KRIS CHRISTENSEN taught creative writing at the Corbin Art Center in Spokane, Washington. In 1999 she received an Artist Trust/Washington State Arts Commission Fellowship in Literature. Her poems have recently appeared in *Portland Review Literary Journal*, *Pontoon: An Anthology of Washington State Poets*, *Hubbub*, *Red Rock Review*, and *Permafrost*.

DAVID CHURA lives in Connecticut and teaches incarcerated high-school students. His essays and poems have appeared in such publications as *New York Times*, *Anthology of New England Writers*, *Turning Wheel*, *English Journal*, and *Essential Love: A Poetry Anthology*. Raised Roman Catholic, he is now a student of vipassana meditation and Buddhism.

TORIA ANGELYN CLARK is a poet and creative writing teacher who lives in Erie, Colorado. Her poem "At Meeting: Where is the Divine in Tragedy?" was written in response to ministry during a Meeting for Worship at the Boulder Friends Meeting (Quakers) and is part of a longer piece titled *Versicolor Chronicle*. Toria has a M.F.A. from Naropa University, and her poems are forthcoming in *Friends Journal, Hard Ground 2000: Writing the Rockies, Bless the Beasts: Children's Prayers & Poems to Honor Animals*, and elsewhere.

ANNE CORAY is a lifelong Alaskan, living on remote Qizhjeh Vena (Lake Clark), her place of birth. *Undated Passages*, her first chapbook, was published through a grant from the Alaska State Council on the Arts. Anne's poems have appeared most recently in *Yefief, Poet Lore, Rhino*, and *Dry Creek Review*. She is dedicated to low-impact living and to furthering environmental consciousness.

KAREN CRAIGO teaches composition at Bowling Green State University in Ohio, and is poetry editor of *Mid-American Review*. Her work has appeared or is forthcoming in *Quarterly West, Another Chicago Magazine, Cimarron Review*, and other publications.

RACHEL DACUS's work has appeared in *Alsop Review, Atlanta Review, Bitter Oleander, Conspire, Portland Review*, and *Switched-On Gutenberg*. Her first poetry collection, *Earth Lessons*, was published by Bellowing Ark Press in 1998 and her work was included in the anthology *Ravishing DisUnities: Real Ghazals in English* (Wesleyan University Press). She resides in the San Francisco Bay Area.

BARBARA DANIELS's chapbook, *The Woman Who Tries to Believe*, won the Quentin R. Howard Prize from Wind Publications. Her poems have appeared in *Massachusetts Review, Seattle Review, Poet Lore*, and *Slant*, as well as elsewhere. She has received an Individual Artist Fellowship from the New Jersey State Council on the Arts and completed an M.F.A. in poetry at Vermont College.

TODD DAVIS is associate professor of English at Goshen College in Goshen, Indiana, where he teaches nature writing, film, and American literature. His poems have appeared in numerous literary reviews, including *Natural Bridge, Worcester Review, Red Cedar Review, Yankee, Farmer's Market, Appalachia, Blueline, Journal of Kentucky Studies*, and *Image: A Journal of the Arts & Religion*.

MARY KRANE DERR is a multiply disabled poet of Roman Catholic/Protestant/Irish/English/Polish/German descent. She lives in Chicago with her teacher husband and actress daughter. She recently completed her first chapbook, *Coming To*. Her work has appeared in such magazines as *Coyote, Ruah*, and *Pudding* and on the Hospice Poetry Recording Project CD *Conversing With Mystery*. This work is part of a poem cycle she presented at the 1999 Parliament of the World's Religions, Cape Town, South Africa, which she dedicated to the Chicago-area Friends of Bede Griffiths and to the nearly forty sponsors of her trip to the Parliament.

CAROLYN DILLE is a poet, food writer, and long-time practitioner in Buddhist meditation. Her poems have appeared in *Montserrat Review*, *Wallace Stevens Journal*, *Practice of Peace*, and other venues. She has published several award-winning books on food and cooking and many articles in magazines such as *Gourmet*, *Food and Wine*, and the *Herb Companion*.

EMORY ELKINS received his B.A. from Fairmont State College and his M.F.A. from Naropa University. He currently lives in downtown Baltimore, where he spends time with his family, writes, and works. His most recent publications include the on-line literary 'zine *Stirring*, and New Orleans-based *Fell Swoop*.

JIM ELLEDGE's many books include his novel in prose poems, *The Chapters of Coming Forth by Day*, which is due soon from Stonewall, a division of BrickHouse, and a limited edition of his long poem, "A Letter to No One, Who Is Named The Past, and the Thoughts That Interrupted the Writing of It" due from Street Lamp Press. His other books include *Gay, Lesbian, Bisexual, and Transgender Myths from the Acoma to the Zuñi* (forthcoming from Peter Lang) and *An Architecture of the Invisible: An Anthology of Poetry by Gays and Lesbians from Precolonial Native America and Hawaii to the End of World War II* (forthcoming from Indiana University Press). His poetry has appeared most recently in *Indiana Review,* which also included an interview with him.

REBECCA MORGAN FRANK teaches yoga, and is pursuing a graduate degree in creative writing.

RAY GONZALEZ is a poet, essayist and editor born in El Paso, Texas. He is the author of two memoirs, seven books of poetry, a book of fiction and a book of essays. His poetry has appeared in the 1999 and 2000 editions of *The Best American Poetry* and *The Pushcart Prize: Best of the Small Presses 2000*. He is the editor of twelve anthologies, served as Poetry Editor for *The Bloomsbury Review* and founded a new poetry journal, *LUNA*.

JEFF GUNDY teaches English at Bluffton College in Ohio. He has published three books of poems, most recently *Rhapsody with Dark Matter* (Bottom Dog, 2000), and *A Community of Memory* (creative nonfiction).

KAREN GUZMAN has published short stories in various literary journals, winning third place in *Bananafish*'s short fiction contest. She is currently at work on a short story collection. She holds an M.F.A. degree from George Mason University and is a staff writer at *The Hartford Courant* in Connecticut.

JULIE JORDAN HANSON's poems have appeared in *The Iowa Review*, *The Journal*, *Michigan Quarterly Review*, and other journals. Her book, in some of its various revisions, has twice been a finalist in the National Poetry Series and a semi-finalist in at least four other competitions. She has an M.A. in expository writing and an M.F.A. in poetry writing from the University of Iowa. She has lived in Iowa now for 23 years, where she helps sustain the household through labor-intensive economies: growing and preserving food and medicinal herbs, milling, and sewing. "Practice" came during a fellowship from the National Endowment for the Arts.

LOIS MARIE HARROD's sixth book of poetry *Spelling the World Backward* has just been published by Palanquin Press, University of South Carolina Aiken, the company that published her chapbook *This Is a Story You Already Know*

(1999) and her book *Part of the Deeper Sea* (1997). Her poems have appeared in many journals, including *American Poetry Review*, *The Carolina Quarterly*, *Southern Poetry Review*, *American Pen*, *Prairie Schooner*, and *Poems & Plays*. Earlier publications include the books *Every Twinge a Verdict* (Belle Mead Press, 1987), *Crazy Alice* (Belle Mead Press, 1991), and a chapbook *Green Snake Riding* (New Spirit Press, 1994). She received 1993 and 1998 fellowship from the New Jersey Council of the Arts for her poetry.

CYNTHIA HOGUE has published three collections of poetry, including *Flux* (New Issues Press, 2002), and has co-edited an anthology of essays on women's avant-garde writing titled *We Who Love To Be Astonished: Experimental Women's Writing and Performance Poetics* (University of Alabama Press, 2001). She has lived and taught in Iceland, Arizona, New Orleans, and New York. She lives in Pennsylvania, where she directs the Stadler Center for Poetry and teaches English at Bucknell University.

AILISH HOPPER graduated from Bennington's M.F.A. program where she received the Jane Kenyon Scholarship. Her poems were published in a special edition of *Poetry Kanto*, edited by Leza Lowitz, on emerging American poets. She lives in Baltimore, Maryland.

ELIZABETH HOWARD has an M.A. in English from Vanderbilt University and taught high school English for several years. She writes both poetry and fiction. Her work has been published in *Xavier Review*, *Visions*, *Cumberland Poetry Review*, *The Comstock Review*, and other journals. She has a poetry book entitled *Anemones*.

VICENTE HUIDOBRO was the father of the Cubist aesthetic Creacionismo, a poetics that strives to create new things by transforming the elements from life into a fresh and independent existence of their own. With Pierre Reverdy, the Chilean-born poet helped form the Parisian avant-garde journal *Nord-Sud*. He then established a literary salon in Madrid and over the next 30 years published poetry in French and Spanish, including his best-known work, *Altazor*. He was 55 when he died in Santiago in 1948. Later that year, his daughter published the work of his final years in his last book, *Ultimos Poemas*.

MARK IRWIN's poetry has appeared in many literary magazines, including *Antaeus*, *American Poetry Review*, *Atlantic*, *Kenyon Review*, *Paris Review*, *The Nation*, and *New England Review*. His most recent book is *White City* (BOA Editions, Ltd., 2000). He is the author of three previous collections: *The Halo of Desire* (Galileo Press, 1987); *Against the Meanwhile: 3 Elegies* (Wesleyan University Press, 1988); and *Quick Now, Always* (BOA Editions, Ltd., 1996). He has translated two volumes of poetry. Recognition for his work includes a "Discovery"/*The Nation* Award, two Pushcart Prizes, National Endowment for the Arts and Ohio Arts Council fellowships, a Fullbright Fellowship to Romania, and a Colorado Recognition for Literature Award.

GORDON JOHNSTON's essays, stories, and poems have appeared or are forthcoming in *The Georgia Review*, *Denver Quarterly*, *American Fiction*, *New Millenium Writings*, *Fourth Genre*, *Wilshire Review*, and other magazines. He is seeking a publisher for his novel *New Moon*. He teaches creative writing and contemporary poetry and fiction at Mercer University in Macon, Georgia, where he directs the Georgia Poetry Circuit.

MARILYN KALLET directs the Creative Writing Program at the University of Tennessee, Knoxville. She is the author of eight books, including three volumes of poetry, the most recent of which is *How to Get Heat Without Fire*. With Judith Ortiz Cofer, she co-edited a volume of personal essays, *Sleeping With One Eye Open: Women Writers and the Art of Survival* (University of Georgia Press, 1999). Kallet's poetry received Honorable Mention in the Anna Davidson Rosenberg contest for poems on the Jewish Experience, sponsored by the Judah I. Magnes Museum in 2000. "Ode to Nelly Sachs" was commissioned for the East Tennessee Conference on the Holocaust, held at the University of Tennessee in March 2001.

THOMAS E. KENNEDY's thirteen books include five works of fiction (most recently the story collection *Drive Dance & Fight* from University of Missouri, Kansas City), four of literary criticism (most notably book length studies of Andre Dubus and Robert Coover from Macmillan), and four anthologies (most recently *Poems & Sources*, which he guest-edited as a special issue of *Literary Review*, including poems and essays by thirty-one poets, including John Updike, Maxine Kumin, Carolyn Kizer, Eavan Boland and many others) and a collection of essays on the craft of fiction, *Realism & Other Illusions*, by Wordcraft of Oregon. His stories, essays, poems, interviews, reviews, translations from the Danish, and photographs appear regularly in North American and European periodicals and anthologies, including the *Pushcart* (1990) and *O Henry* (1994) volumes. He lives in Denmark and serves as Advisory Editor to *Literary Review*.

ANYA KRUGOVOY teaches English and directs the Women's and Gender Studies Program at Mercer University. Her poetry has recently appeared in *North American Review*, *Poet Lore*, *Laurel Review*, *Cream City Review*, and other literary magazines. She lives with her husband in Macon, Georgia.

JOSEPH W. KRUSINSKI has worked as an independent marketing consultant for a wide array of retail, industrial, professional, and medical clients. As a graphic designer, illustrator and copywriter, he has produced many successful marketing collateral pieces, and recently decided to actively pursue his love of creating fine art, which includes commissioned oil portraits, as well as the cover of this journal.

STEVE LANGAN's collection of poems, *Freezing*, was published by New Issues Press of Western Michigan University. Other poems from the collection have appeared in *Doubletake*, *Kenyon Review*, *Colorado Review*, *Chicago Review*, *Witness*, *Southern Humanities Review*, *Cutbank*, and other journals.

JUDITH LAVEZZI is a writer and long-time ponderer of the idiosyncrasies of our human lives. She has been attempting to write down those thoughts and observations since her childhood in Chicago. This is her first submission to any publication.

JOYANNA LAUGHLIN is an author, poet, and journalist with an M.F.A. from Naropa University in Boulder, Colorado. Her fiction has appeared in the anthology *Jumbo Shrimp* and in the literary journal *Elixir*, and she is currently working on a novel. Her business and environmental journalism appears regularly in such publications as *Natural Home*, *Natural Business*, and *LOHAS (Lifestyles of Health and Sustainability) Journal*, and she was research assistant for *The Colorado Weather Book* (Westcliffe Publishers, 1999). Joyanna lives in Estes Park, Colorado, with her husband, John, a dog, and two cats.

NAOMI RUTH LOWINSKY lived in India as a young woman. Her western consciousness was cracked open by the wild tumult of Hindu divinities and devotions, and she stumbled upon what would become her spiritual path, leading her to poetry and Jungian psychology. She has recently published an essay on all this, "The Fire of India," in *Psychological Perspectives*. Her poetry has been published in numerous publications including *Earth's Daughters*, *Paterson Literary Review*, *American Writing*, *Small Pond* and *Baybury Review*. She is a Jungian Analyst in practice in Berkeley, California, and Poetry and Fiction Editor of *Psychological Perspectives*, a journal that is published by the Los Angeles Jung Institute.

CHRISTOPHER LUNA is a poet, editor, journalist, and performer with an M.F.A. in Writing and Poetics from the Jack Kerouac School of Disembodied Poetics at the Naropa University in Boulder, Colorado. His articles and criticism have appeared in the *Island Ear*, *Rain Taxi*, the *Boulder Planet*, the *Colorado Daily*, and Brain-juice.com. His poetry has appeared in publications including *Gare du Nord*, *Exquisite Corpse*, *Babylon Review*, *Depths of a Greyhound Terminal*, *Through the Looking Glass*, *Gates of Dawn*, *Gumball Poetry*, and *Big Scream*. Luna has collaborated with musicians including Dystopia One, Pimpcore, Liquid Logic, Piltdown Man, Vole, and Steven Taylor. He is currently editing the selected correspondence of the filmmaker Stan Brakhage and Michael McClure.

ROBERT MANASTER lives and works in Champaign, Illinois. His poetry has appeared or will appear in *Image: A Journal of the Arts & Religion*, *JUDAISM*, *Wisconsin Review*, and other publications. He has been a finalist in the Nicholas Roerich Poetry Competition (Story Line Press) and the Headwaters Literary Competition (New Rivers Press).

MEREDITH MCGHAN moved from Ann Arbor, Michigan to Las Vegas to attend the M.F.A. program in creative writing at UNLV. Her freelance reviews have appeared in *What's On!*, *Zap2it.com*, and other venues. Her poetry has appeared in *Free Focus* and *Lime Green Bulldozers*. She has taught creative expression workshops to "at-risk" youth, participated at a variety of performance venues, and worked many day jobs which have given her a warped and spiritually eclectic view of reality.

KATE MCHENRY has spent many years seeking new metaphors for the spiritual journey. She has a Ph.D. in religion and currently is teaching American Studies. Her poems have appeared in a wide variety of magazines and journals, including *Alive Now!*, *Daughters of Sarah*, *Embers*, *Footwork*, *Metis*, *Other Side*, and *Witness*.

FELICIA MITCHELL's chapbook *Earthenware Fertility Figure* won first place in a recent Talent House Press contest. "Diasporo" is from a collection called *My Book of Ruth*. Felicia teaches at Emory & Henry College.

DORU MOTZ is a broadcaster, producer, and simultaneous interpreter for the Voice of America in Washington, DC, as well as a writer and a typographer/designer of fonts. He has published over forty books and translated thousands of technical and informational articles for corporations, translation agencies, the U.S. Navy and Department of Justice, as well as (on a daily basis) the VOA. He has not done much literary translation, though he is currently working on an English version of *Requiem for Madmen and Beasts*, fiction by the important Romanian novelist, Augustin Buzura.

PETER E. MURPHY's poetry is in recent issues of *Commonweal*, *Confrontation*, *Cortland Review*, *Cream City Review*, *Many Mountains Moving*, *Mudlark*, *Slipstream*, and *World Order*. Two poems are also included in *Outsiders: Poems about Rebels, Exiles, and Renegades* and *Urban Nature: Poems about Wildlife in the City* both recently published by Milkweed. He is a consultant to the Geraldine R. Dodge Foundation's poetry program and has been an educational advisor to a number of PBS television series on poetry including *Fooling with Words* with Bill Moyers that was broadcast last year. He also wrote a series of poetry lessons for teachers that is online at www.pbs.org/foolingwithwords. He teaches English and creative writing at Atlantic City High School and directs the Winter Poetry & Prose Getaway held annually in Cape May.

ROBENS NAPOLITAN is a regular participant in Sandpoint, Idaho's open-mike venue called "Five Minutes of Fame." She is also a member of the Sandpoint Writers Collective, a group that meets weekly to write extemporaneously. Her work has appeared in *Orphic Lute*, *cold-drill*, and *Heliotrope*. She lives by a lake with Tom, her husband of twenty-five years, and their cat, Muffin. In addition to writing, her greatest love is interacting with nature.

BEA OPENGART's poems have appeared in a number of journals, including *American Voice*, *Apalachee Quarterly*, *Louisville Review*, *Ohio Journal*, and others. Her collection, *Erotica*, was published by Owl Creek Press. Bea teaches at University of Cincinnati in Ohio.

BETH PARTIN is the author of *Microgravity*, a novel published by Livingston Press at the University of West Alabama in June 1998. She is currently working on a collection of short stories and revising a novel, *What You Asked For*. She has had poems accepted for publication in *Grasslands Review*, *Ledge*, and *Clackamas Review*.

GERRYE PAYNE's books and chapbooks of poetry include *The Year-God*, Ahsahta Press, 1992, *A Sampler*, Clamshell Press, 1998, and *The Silence of Arvo Pärt, A Modest Proposal Chapbook*, July, 2000. Her poems have appeared in many journals, most recently in *Commonweal*, *Fishdrum*, *Karamu*, and *Primavera*. She lives in western Sonoma County in Northern California.

CARLOS PELLICER (d. 1977) was a museum director, social activist, and one of the important Mexican poets of the twentieth century. His poems are translated from *Material Poético, 1918-1961* with the gracious permission of the publisher, the Universidad Nacional Autunoma de Mexico.

JUDITH PORDON resides in Paso Ancho, Jalisco, Mexico, where most of her first drafts are written, and San Diego, California, where revisions are made. Her poetry can be seen in the anthology, *Tri-verse City* (1999 Austin International Poetry Festival Anthology) and in current or upcoming issues of *The Ledge*, *Writers' Journal*, *Impetus*, and online at *2River View*, *Agnieskas Dowry*, *ForPoetry.com*, *Comrades*, *Stirring*, and *Recursive Angel*.

LARA RAMSEY, originally from Washington State, is a student in the M.F.A. program at the University of Nevada Las Vegas. Previous poems have been published in *Synapse*, *Crosscurrents*, and *Café Dialogue*.

LEN ROBERTS has published seven books of poetry, including *The Trouble-Making Finch* (1998) and *Counting the Black Angels* (1994), both from the University of Illinois Press. His book of poetry, *The Silent Singer: New and Selected Poems*, was published by University of Illinois Press in 2001.

DEBORAH ROBSON studied writing as an undergraduate at the Universities of Iowa and Washington, and earned her M.F.A. in fiction in the earliest years of the Goddard/Warren Wilson program. Her short stories, essays, articles, and book reviews have appeared in more than fifteen magazines and three anthologies. Like many other Quakers (also known as "seekers"), she discovers a great deal of her spirituality in daily activities. She's learned lots about strength through her relationship with her daughter.

VALERIE ROBLES works for Kimco Staffing Services in Riverside, California, and recently has had work published in *White Pelican Review*.

ADRIENNE ROSS is a writer, naturalist, and grant writer living in Seattle, Washington. Her essays have appeared in *Tikkun*, *Northern Lights*, *New Age Journal*, the anthology *Intricate Weave: Women Write on Girls and Girlhood*, the American Nature Writing anthology series, and numerous other publications.

DOROTHY RYAN is a poet and teacher. Her poems have appeared in *Paterson Literary Review*, *Black Buzzard Review*, and others. She has work forthcoming in *Impetus*, *Parting Gifts,* and *America*. She lives in New Jersey with her husband, daughter, and their black lab. Her strong belief in a higher power sustains her, and communing with the wildlife on her property enriches her spirit.

WILLA SCHNEBERG received an Oregon Literary Arts Fellowship in Poetry and a Money for Women/Barbara Deming Memorial Fund Grant in Poetry. Poems have recently appeared in *American Poetry Review* and in the anthologies: *Points of Contact: Disability, Art, and Culture*, University of Michigan Press, *Knowing Stones: Poems of Exotic Places*, John Gordon Burke Inc. and will appear in a textbook *To Remember: Teaching The Holocaust*, Heinemann. Her photographs of Khmer Buddhist Nuns have been in the pages of *Tricycle: The Buddhist Review* and *Bombay Gin*.

MARTIN SCOTT is a writer living in Houston, Texas, where he teaches English at the Houston Community College—Northline Mall Campus. He has creative writing degrees from the University of Iowa (M.F.A.) and the University of Houston (Ph.D.), and he has previously published poems in such journals as *New York Quarterly*, *Southern Poetry Review*, *Plainsongs*, *Drunken Boat*, *Willow Spring*, *Gulf Coast*, *Sow's Ear Poetry Review*, *Tucumcari Literary Review*, *Poet Lore*, and essays in *Blue Mesa Review*, *Under the Sun,* and *Paideuma*. Most recently, he won the Larry Levis Editors' Award for Poetry at *Missouri Review*.

SUSAN SINK teaches creative writing, composition, and non-western literature. She was a Stegner Fellow in Poetry at Stanford University in 1991–1993, and her work has appeared in several national literary magazines.

DONNY SMITH's poems, translations, and articles have appeared in *Ancient Paths*, *Extranjera a la Intemperie*, *Lilliput Review*, *Luz en Arte y Literatura*, and elsewhere. He works at Swarthmore College and edits the poetry magazine *Dwan*.

173

CECILIA SOPRANO is a published illustrator and writer who lives in southeastern Connecticut with her old cat, Houston. She gardens for a living; Houston sleeps. They both dream in color and have visions of a happier world.

ADAM J. SORKIN is a widely published literary translator. His recent volumes include *Sea-Level Zero,* poems by Daniela Crasnaru mostly translated with the poet (BOA Editions, 1999); *Bebop Baby*, by Mircea Cartarescu (Poetry New York series, 1999); and *The Triumph of the Water Witch*, prose poems by Ioana Ieronim translated with the poet (Bloodaxe, 2000). Sorkin is working on a volume of Mihai Ursachi's poetry, *Madness and Light*, partially translated with the poet.

SHERMAN SOUTHER has a M.F.A. in creative writing from Naropa University. He has had a lifelong interest in the Spanish language and its literature.

SETH A. STEINZOR, a lawyer, lives with his wife, a social worker, and their two children in Burlington, Vermont, where, when not working, he makes poems, furniture and bamboo fly fishing rods, plays harmonica in a country western band called Ruby Ditch and the Fabulous Endings, and worships at the stream of his choice. He was born to a secular Jewish academic family in California and grew up near Buffalo, New York.

SCOTT STRUMAN has had poetry published in *Rivertalk*, *Northridge Review*, *Last Tangos*, *Golden Apple Press*, *ARTLIFE*, *Poetry Motel*, *Santa Barbara Independent,* and *Stained Sheets*.

VIRGIL SUÁREZ was born in Havana, Cuba, in 1962. Since 1974, he has lived in the United States. He is the author of four novels, a collection of stories and a memoir that chronicles his life of exile both in Cuba and in the United States. He also is the author of three collections of poetry and the editor of two anthologies. His essays, stories, poems, and translations continue to appear both nationally and internationally in journals and reviews.

MARY SULLIVAN, r.c., has been a Religious of the Cenacle for forty-four years. She has given retreats throughout Europe, Asia, Canada, and the United States. She co-founded the At Home Retreat Movement. She is certified as a spiritual director and mental health counselor. She has co-authored two books for women on prayer, written articles in *Sisters' Today*, *Review for Religious*, and *Human Development*. She is a member of the Cenacle's International Commission on Spirituality.

KATHY KENNEDY TAPP's poetry has appeared in journals and anthologies, including *Wisconsin Academy Review*, *Orion*, and *Earth's Daughters*. She is an editor for *What Canst Thou Say?*, a Quaker newsletter on mystical experiences.

SUSAN THOMAS has published work recently in *Nimrod*, *Columbia*, *Kalliope*, *Crab Orchard Review*, and *Lullwater Review*. New work is forthcoming in *South Carolina Review*, *Atlanta Review*, and *Glimmer Train*, as well as in two anthologies, *9mm* and *Poetry of Exile* (University of Iowa Press). She has won the Editors' Prize from the *Spoon River Poetry Review* and the New York Stories Annual Short Fiction Contest.

ATTICUS JAMES TOLAN entered a seminary years ago and left. He loves a number of people he has only begun to know. He teaches, writes a little, and publishes some, but mostly he tries to stay aware through it all and be one of the people Lorca wrote for, one of the awake. Poems of his have appeared most recently in *Luna*, *Lilliput Review*, *New Digressions*, *Salt Hill Journal*, and the anthology *What Have You Lost?*, edited by Naomi Shihab Nye.

ROSEMERRY WAHTOLA TROMMER lives in Telluride, Colorado, and is a hiker, skier, and optimist. In addition to writing for *Backpacker*, *Mountain Living*, and *Natural Home*, she writes an award-winning linguistics column, directs the Telluride Writers Guild, teaches poetry classes and has published two books of poetry: *lunaria* (Sisu Press, 1999) and *if you listen: poetry & photographs of the san juan mountains* (Western Reflections Press, 2000). She is featured in *Geography of Hope: Poets of Colorado's Western Slope* (Conundrum Press, 1998) and edited *Charity: True Stories of Giving and Receiving* (Red Rock Press, 2001). In 2000, Rosemerry won the National Young Careerist competition sponsored by Business and Professional Women of the United States.

MIHAI URSACHI is one of Romania's most eminent writers.

Translator Adam J. Sorkin writes, "Ursachi is one of Romania's most eminent writers, and, I believe, a major neglected literary figure of world poetry today. His work bodies forth a combination of mysticism, irony and surreal symbolism; the metaphysical intensity of his "poetry of being" (Ursachi's own term for his aesthetic) and his yoking of traditional devices and occasionally old-fangled diction to a contemporary, not infrequently arch manner make his voice both unusual and compelling. "I call myself a reactionary modernist," he once joked to me, an apt description consonant with his self-categorization as an "Orphic poet." Ursachi's biography is a parable for the second half of the twentieth century. He defected from Romania in 1981 after having been caught during an escape attempt as a student two decades before. Prominent in a loose intellectual opposition at the University of Iasi, Ursachi had refused to collaborate with the secret police, and, warned of his imminent arrest, he'd got halfway across the Danube to Yugoslavia when a boat intercepted him. He survived the Romanian gulag only because of a general amnesty three years later; his ordeal included weeks of solitary confinement in a hole in the ground at Romania's most notorious political prison, Jilava, "a place," he has remarked, "where you were expected to die"—not unlike the ordinary world itself, of course, but far more urgent. There in solitary, Ursachi wrote his "very first poem, 'wrote' in memory, that is." For the twenty-year-old intending to be a philosopher, poetry immediately became more than a "real and deep vocation" but also his "only reason to exist" and "a kind of spiritual resistance." Allowed out of the country in 1981 on a USIA grant (once in a while Romania's police state would issue an almost impossible-to-get passport as direct encouragement not to return), Ursachi sought political asylum while in the United States, winding up in California and then Texas. In Austin, he put himself through grad school in German while learning English. Subsequently, he taught part-time at La Jolla for four years. Immediately after the December 1989 revolution that overthrew communism in Romania, Ursachi repatriated, serving until February 1992 as Director of the National Theater in the city of Iasi, the traditional cultural center of the northeastern Romanian region of Moldavia where he was born in 1941. He lost the National Theater post due to his open opposition to the government and his allowing the use of the Theater for an international ceremony commemorating the fiftieth anniversary of the Great Pogrom of Iasi, which a few local officials denied ever took place. In 1992 he was awarded the first national Mihai Eminescu poetry prize since World War II, one of his numerous awards. *Madness and Light*, Mihai Ursachi's twelfth book of poetry, a career retrospective containing over forty new titles, was published in 1998. Currently Professor of Poetry at the Alexandru Ioan Cuza in Iasi, he is commonly addressed as "Magister" by fellow writer, maybe with an occasional hint of wryness but never without deep respect for his literary stature and personal presence. Ursachi remains committed to a poetry founded on philosophy and belief, a sustaining ontology for art and human existence. It is out of this perspective that, despite his many tangible attainments, Ursachi could avow to me in conversation, "When…I knew I was going to die soon in prison, underground, sometimes three meters, sometimes ten meters, and I'd never written a poem, and I'd never had a woman, I was still able to say, 'I am satisfied. This has been my life. I left a little light.'"

KARLA VAN VLIET was born and raised in Vermont. She attended Bennington College and earned her B.A. from Goddard College and her M.F.A. from Vermont College. After extensive travel, she has settled in central Vermont. Her work has appeared in *Painted Bride Quarterly*, *Plainsongs*, *Ship of Fools*, *Eleventh Muse*, and *Dry Creek Review*.

JACK VIAN is a native of Houston, Texas who has studied literature at California State University and the University of Houston. He continues to write poetry, short stories, and novels about a variety of topics.

JOHN VIEIRA has been a practitioner of Adidam (www.adidam.org) since 1975, and serves that organization full-time. Over the past twenty years, ten chapbooks of his poetry have appeared, the most recent of which is *Points on a Hazard Map* (Runaway Spoon, 1999). He lives with his wife Cindy in the Washington, D.C. area, where he freelances in TV news for a living. His essay, "Ecstatic Writing: An Appeal for the Reclamation of Poetry" (*The Bitter Oleander*; vol. 4, no. 1), was nominated for the 1999 Pushcart Prize.

DAVI WALDERS is a poet, writer, and education consultant whose work has appeared in *Cross Currents*, *Liberal Religious Education*, *Midstream*, *Judaism*, and anthologies. She is the recipient of a Time Out for Women Grant from the Association for Religion and Intellectual Life. She developed and directs the Vital Signs Poetry Project at the National Institutes of Health and its Children's Inn in Bethesda, Maryland. She has had residencies at Blue Mountain Center, Ragdale Foundation, Virginia Center for the Creative Arts, and elsewhere.

KEN WALDMAN, a past contributor to *Many Mountains Moving*, has had recent work published in *Arts & Letters* and *Puerto del Sol*. A freelance writer and teacher, he also tours as Alaska's Fiddling Poet. His first full-length collection, *Nome Poems*, is available from West End Press, and his second, *To Live on This Earth*, is due out in early 2002. His CD, *A Week in Eek*, has received wide national airplay. He lives in Anchorage.

G. C. WALDREP has had previous work published in *Poetry*, *Ascent*, *South Carolina Review*, and other journals. His book, *Southern Workers and the Search for Community*, is available from University of Illinois Press. From 1995 to 2000, he lived in the New Order Amish settlement at Yanceyville, North Carolina.

Good News About Contributors

TONY HOAGLAND's poetry collection, *Donkey Gospel*, is available from Graywolf Press (ISBN 1-55597-268-3). His book is winner of the James Laughlin Award of The Academy of American Poets. Hungry Mind Review writes, "Tony Hoagland's puzzlement is palpable, and yet his effervescent cleverness and original twists of phrase, sometimes aphoristic in philosophical content, ring true."

B.D. LOVE's book of poetry, *Water at the Women's Edge*, is available from Urthona Press (ISBN 0-9648305-3-6). "What gratitude and astonishment I feel at reading B. D. Love's poetry.... Love's women's monologues and meditations are both lyrical and disturbing in their unceasing honesty, as though as tender as the lives he's celebrating," writes Amy Uyematsu, author of *Nights of Fire, Nights of Rain*, of his book. To order, e-mail urthona1@aol.com.

PAMELA USCHUK's poetry collection, *Finding Peaches in the Desert*, is available from Wings Press (ISBN 0-930324-59-5). Joy Harjo describes this book: "These poems make a sensual garden.... There is singing in this garden, and though it might be the end of the world, a new world is coming into view, just over the horizon of these poems." Check the Web at www.wingspress.com or phone (21)271-7805 to order.

MMM ORDER / SPONSORSHIP FORM

Two-issue subscriptions are $16 ($29 for four-issue subscription)*,**. Gift subscriptions make a perfect gift. The first issue of gift subscriptions will be sent with a card in your name. If you are not completely satisfied, we will promptly send you a refund.

*Canada add $3.00 to each single issue or $6.00 per 2-issue subscription. *Other countries add $5.00 to each single issue or $10.00 per 2-issue subscription.*

** *Colorado residents add ONE of the following tax amounts for journal purchases: Boulder—7.36%; Denver Metro—3.7%; CO outside of Denver area—2.9%.*

Please begin my subscription with ❏ **the current issue (#13) /** ❏ **next issue (check one)**

Subscriber's name _____ Subscriptions (circle one)

Street/Apt. No. _____

City/State/Zip _____ $16 for 2 issues

Phone _____ $29 for 4 issues

   $44 for 6 issues $_____

Gift subscriptions:

Recipient's name _____ Gift subscriptions (circle one)

Street/Apt. No. _____

City/State/Zip _____ $16 for 2 issues

Sender's name _____ $29 for 4 issues

Sender's addr/phone _____ $44 for 6 issues $_____

❏ **Yes, I would also like to order individual issues of Many Mountains Moving**

Inaugural issue, #2, #3, #4, #7, #8, #9, #10
(circle requested issue #s) ___ @ $6.00 each $_____

Tribute to W.S. Merwin (#11) ___ @ $9.00 each $_____

Issue #12 ___ @ $9.00 each $_____

Literaure of Spirituality (Vol. IV, No. 3, current) ___ @ $9.00 each $_____

Additional charge for foreign purchases* $_____

Subtotal $_____

Colorado tax** $_____

Become a sponsor. We invite you to become a sponsor of Many Mountains Moving by making a tax-deductible contribution (contributions are tax-deductible minus the $16 value of the 2 issues). Sponsors receive a two-issue subscription to the journal and will be recognized in those issues for their contributions.

❏ **Supporting subscriber ($30)** ❏ **Donor ($50)** ❏ **Patron ($100)** ❏ **Benefactor ($250)**

Tax-deductible sponsorship donation $_____

Total amount enclosed $_____

Send check or money order to:
Many Mountains Moving, 420 22nd St., Boulder, CO 80302 U.S.A.

Phone (303)545-9942; Fax (303)444-6510
mmm@mmminc.org
www.mmminc.org

MĀNOA

Seeking the unexpected? You'll find it in this beautiful, ground-breaking journal—writers from Japan, the Philippines, New Zealand, Australia, Viet Nam, Korea, and the rest of the international Pacific and Asia...including the United States. *"Vitality and surprise"*—W. S. Merwin. *"Access to some of the best voices in world literature"*—Small Press. **Visit our website at www2.hawaii.edu/mjournal and see why** MĀNOA **is unlike any other American journal.**

Published every summer and winter by the University of Hawaiʻi Press, 2840 Kolowalu St., Honolulu, HI 96822. TOLL-FREE TEL 1-888-UHPRESS / TOLL-FREE FAX 1-800-650-7811 / E-MAIL mjournal-l@hawaii.edu.

CONGRATULATIONS

to the following winners of the third annual
Many Mountains Moving
Literary Awards!

Janet McAdams (poetry)
Catherine Elizabeth Puckett (fiction)
James Van Amber (nonfiction)

Their award-winning entries will be
featured in the next issue.

Upcoming Contributors

Nature Issue, edited by Brian Andrew Laird and Luis Urrea
Special Generations Issue
William Aiken
Steve Bradbury
Natasha Bruckner
Michael Calvello
Dana Curtis
Paul Eggers
Maria Gillan
Sharon Hashimoto
Michael Henry
Felix Jung
Brian Andrew Laird
Jeffrey Levine
Mari L'Esperance
Wendell Mayo
Joshua McKinney
Orlando Ricardo Menes
Martin Naparsteck
Veronica Patterson
Joel Peckham, Jr.
Jody Rambo
Marge Piercy
Richard Siken
Adam Sol
Virgil Suárez
Luis Alberto Urrea
Jay Veazey
Eve Wood
Hsia Yu